Teaching the Common Core Literature Standards in Grades 2–5

Shifting your literature instruction to meet the Common Core can be tricky. The standards are specific about how students should analyze characters, themes, points of view, and more. In this new book, Lisa Morris makes it easy by taking you through the standards and offering tons of practical strategies, tools, and mentor texts for grades 2–5. She shows you how to combine the standards into effective units of study so that you can teach with depth rather than worry about coverage. Topics covered include:

- teaching questioning, inferring, and author's purpose;
- guiding readers to look at themes and write summaries;
- showing students how to recognize structural elements of literature;
- teaching the craft of writing and vocabulary development; and
- helping students analyze characters and character development.

Throughout this highly practical book, you'll find a variety of charts and other graphic organizers that can be easily adapted for classroom use. A list of suggested mentor texts is also available as a free eResource from our website, www.routledge.com/9781138856172.

Lisa Morris is a language arts teacher at Bluewater Elementary in Niceville, Florida and Adjunct Professor of Education at Northwest Florida State College. She is also author of *Awakening Brilliance in the Writer's Workshop: Using Notebooks, Mentor Texts, and the Writing Process* (Routledge, 2012).

Other Eye On Education Books Available from Routledge (www.routledge.com/eyeoneducation)

Awakening Brilliance in the Writer's Workshop Using Notebooks, Mentor Texts, and the Writing Process
Lisa Morris

**Closing Reading in Elementary School:
Bringing Readers and Texts Together**
Diana Sisson and Betsy Sisson

**Focus on Text:
Tackling the Common Core Reading Standards,
Grades 4–8**
Amy Benjamin

**Nonfiction Strategies That Work:
Do This—Not That!**
Lori G. Wilfong

**Vocabulary Strategies That Work:
Do This—Not That!**
Lori G. Wilfong

**Writing Strategies That Work:
Do This—Not That!**
Lori G. Wilfong

**The Common Core Grammar Toolkit:
Using Mentor Texts to Teach the Language Standards
in Grades 3–5**
Sean Ruday

**The Informational Writing Toolkit:
Using Mentor Texts in Grades 3–5**
Sean Ruday

Family Reading Night, 2nd Edition
Darcy J. Hutchins, Joyce L. Epstein, and Marsha D. Greenfeld

Teaching the Common Core Literature Standards in Grades 2–5

Strategies, Mentor Texts, and Units of Study

Lisa Morris

Routledge
Taylor & Francis Group
NEW YORK AND LONDON

First published 2016
by Routledge
605 Third Avenue, New York, NY 10017

and by Routledge
2 Park Square, Milton Park, Abingdon, Oxon, OX14 4RN

Routledge is an imprint of the Taylor & Francis Group, an informa business

© 2016 Taylor & Francis

The right of Lisa Morris to be identified as author of this work has been asserted by her in accordance with sections 77 and 78 of the Copyright, Designs and Patents Act 1988.

All rights reserved. No part of this book may be reprinted or reproduced or utilised in any form or by any electronic, mechanical, or other means, now known or hereafter invented, including photocopying and recording, or in any information storage or retrieval system, without permission in writing from the publishers.

Trademark notice: Product or corporate names may be trademarks or registered trademarks, and are used only for identification and explanation without intent to infringe.

Library of Congress Cataloging-in-Publication Data
Morris, Lisa, 1969–.
 Teaching the common core literature standards in grades 3–5: strategies, mentor texts, and units of study/Lisa Morris.
 pages cm
 Includes bibliographical references.
 1. Reading (Elementary)—United States. 2. Literature—Study and teaching (Elementary)—United States. 3. Content area reading. 4. Common Core State Standards (Education) I. Title.
 LB1573.M65 2015
 372.4—dc23
 2015002724

ISBN: 978-1-138-85616-5 (hbk)
ISBN: 978-1-138-85617-2 (pbk)
ISBN: 978-1-315-71985-6 (ebk)

Typeset in Palatino and Formata
by Florence Production Ltd, Stoodleigh, Devon, UK

Contents

Meet the Author ix

1 **Embracing the Language of the Standards and Creating a Curriculum** 1
    General Information about the Common Core State Standards 1
    An Overview of the Reading Standards for Literature 5
    Explaining My Methodology 7
    Using "I Can" Statements 11
    It Takes a Village 12
    Units of Study: Depth not Coverage 16
    Content Area Reading 18
    Resources for Teachers 19
    Common Core Resources 19
    Choice Boards 20
    Closing Thoughts 21

2 **Questioning, Inferring, and Author's Purpose: A Likely Trio for Comprehension** 22
    I Can Statements 22
    Questioning and Inferring—Intertwining the Two 23
    Generic Organizers for Responding to Reading 31
    Asking Questions 35
    Mentor Texts for Questioning 39
    Going Deeper Within the Study 42
    What is a Prediction? 43
    Mentor Texts for Predicting 46
    What is an Inference? 46
    Inferring with Poetry, Pictures, and Wordless Books 51
    Mentor Texts for Poetry 55
    The Power of Pictures 55

	A Closer Look at Author's Purpose 59
	Choice Board 62
	Closing Thoughts. 62
3	**Guiding Students to Write Sensational Summaries and Recognize Themes** 63
	I Can Statements 63
	The Importance of Summarizing 64
	Summarizing vs. Retelling. 66
	Determining Importance 67
	Summarizing to Evaluate Comprehension 70
	Looking Closer at Themes 81
	Additional Ways to Teach Themes. 85
	Thematic Conflict. 87
	Excellent Resources for Implementing a Genre Study 91
	Choice Board 94
	Closing Thoughts. 94
4	**Reading with Close Comprehension Through Character Analysis and Story Elements** 95
	I Can Statements 95
	Character Analysis. 96
	Mentor Texts and Author Choices 97
	Possible Mini-Lessons for Character Analysis 98
	Cause and Effect 134
	Organizers for Documenting Cause and Effect Relationships. 136
	Choice Board 140
	Closing Thoughts. 140
5	**Reading Closely to Recognize the Importance of Craft and Vocabulary Development** 141
	I Can Statements 141
	The Craft of Writing 142
	Teaching Students to Notice Craft of Language. 145
	Four Categories of Craft. 145
	Activities and Mentor Texts for Teaching Word Craft 147
	Graphic Organizers for Modeled and Intendant Reading 152
	Activities and Mentor Texts for Teaching Audible Craft 168
	Tying in Vivid Vocabulary. 173

    Graphic Organizers to Aid Vocabulary Study 178
    Monitoring the Mood and Tone 184
    Identifying the Author's Tone or Mood. 186
    Connecting with Illustrations 187
    Choice Board 189
    Closing Thoughts. 189

6 Recognizing the Structural Elements of Prose, Poetry, and Drama 190
    I Can Statements 190
    Comparing Prose, Poetry, and Drama. 191
    Teaching Students to be Pros at Prose 196
    Poetry. 198
    Rhythm 200
    Digging Drama. 202
    Point of View 204
    Choice Board 211
    Closing Thoughts. 211

---

eResources

Suggestions for mentor texts are available as a free eResource on our website so you can easily print and copy it for your own use.

Go to the book's product page,

    www.routledge.com/9781138856172

Then click on the tab that says eResources. The eResource will begin downloading to your computer.

Meet the Author

Lisa Morris teaches ELA at Bluewater Elementary in Niceville, Florida. She has been an educator for 25 years. She also conducts writing workshops for the teachers in her district. Lisa holds a Master's in Early Childhood Education from Lagrange College. She was nominated as the 2009–2010 Teacher of the Year for her previous school, Edge Elementary. For the past 2 years, she has also been an adjunct professor of education at Northwest Florida State College. Lisa spends much of her time writing, at the beach with her family, and teaching. Her web site is *www.lisamorriswrites.com*.

Lisa has published several other books, stories, and articles. These include:

- *Powerful Persuasive Writing* (Tate Publishing, June 2015)
- *Expository Explosion* (Tate Publishing, March 2015)
- *The Dog Did WHAT?* (Chicken Soup for the Soul, 2014)
- *Reboot Your Life* (Chicken Soup for the Soul, 2014)
- *Narrative Know-How* (Tate Publishing, 2014)
- *One Life at a Time: A Rescuer's Memoir* (CreateSpace, May 2014)
- *Snippets: An Anthology of Small Moments, Scraps of Thoughts and Bits of Advice* (CreateSpace, April 2014)
- *Saving Anabelle* (Pixelhose, February 2014)
- *RTI Meets Writer's Workshop* (Corwin Press, February 2013)
- *Awakening Brilliance in the Writer's Workshop* (Routledge, 2012)
- *Chicken Soup for the Soul: The Gift of Christmas: Bones for Christmas* (December 2010)
- *Chicken Soup for the Soul: My Dog's Life: Room for One More* (April 2011)
- Heartwarmers: *Buttermilk Biscuits and Sun-dried Apple Treats* (July 2010)
- Just Labs magazine: *"Are We Talking Belly Buttons Here?"* (July 2010)
- Thematic Unit: Awesome Aussies, The Education Center
- Thematic Unit: Fabulous Food, Frank Schaffer Publication

Chapter 1

Embracing the Language of the Standards and Creating a Curriculum

"If you are going to get anywhere in life you have to read a lot of books."

Roald Dahl

General Information about the Common Core State Standards

The Common Core State Standards (CCSS) are an effort by educators to define a base knowledge of skills that students should develop in grades K-12. The underlying goal of the standards is for students to graduate from high school prepared for college and careers. Additional information is available on the CCSS website (www.corestandards.org).

If you are an educator, principal, or other educational professional, you know about the Common Core State Standards. For the past 3 years, these standards have been the root of many a faculty meeting, collegial discussion, workshop, etc. It is my goal, with this book, not to teach teachers about the standards, but how to effectively use and understand the standards. Educators have a wide assortment of valuable lessons, resources, and activities that have been proven effective in teaching. This is not the time to reinvent the wheel, rather a time to dig a little deeper and with a confident conviction that the standards will not dominate teaching, rather enhance it.

The goals of this book are to:

1. review the standards and key shifts for ELA;
2. correlate the standards in grades 2–5 to create a spiral curriculum for Reading Literature;
3. show effective ways to organize teaching materials into units of study;
4. provide lessons, ideas, suggestions, mentor text lists, and activities that will help classroom teachers with prescriptive planning;
5. recognize the importance of the craft and structure of texts.

Key Shifts for English Language Arts and Literacy

- **Shift 1: Balancing Informational & Literary Text**

    Students read a true balance of informational and literary texts.

- **Shift 2: Knowledge in the Disciplines**

    Students build knowledge about the world (domains/content areas) through TEXT rather than solely by the teacher.

- **Shift 3: Staircase of Complexity**

    Students read the central, grade-appropriate text around which instruction is centered. Teachers are patient, create more time and space and support in the curriculum for close reading.

- **Shift 4: Text-based Answers**

    Students engage in rich and rigorous evidence-based conversations about text.

- **Shift 5: Writing from Sources**

    Writing emphasizes use of evidence from sources to inform or make an argument.

- **Shift 6: Academic Vocabulary**

    Students constantly build the transferable vocabulary they need to access grade-level complex texts. This can be done effectively by spiraling like content in increasingly complex texts.

Key Features of the Standards

- **Reading: Text complexity and growth of comprehension**

  The reading standards place equal emphasis on the complexity of what students read and the skill with which they read.

- **Writing: Text types, responding to reading, and research**

  The writing standards acknowledge the fact that while some writing skills (e.g., the ability to plan, revise, edit, and publish) apply to many types of writing, other skills relate to specific types of writing: arguments, informative/explanatory texts, and narratives.

- **Speaking and listening: Flexible communication and collaboration**

  The speaking and listening standards require students to develop a range of broadly useful oral communication and interpersonal skills, not just skills needed for formal presentations.

- **Language: Conventions (grammar), effective use, and vocabulary**

  The language standards include the essential "rules" of standard written and spoken English, but they also look at language as a matter of craft and making choices.

Common Concerns of the Standards

Let's face it, when first introduced, the Common Core did not make educators feel warm and cozy. As time went by, more and more opposition seemed to surface. There was a good reason for the concerns. Change feels uncomfortable sometimes. After reading article after article on the pros and cons of this new educational movement, I found that a few common concerns among most of what I read were:

1. **The CCSS would standardize instruction and eliminate creativity in the classrooms.**

   My Thoughts: Teachers are dedicated and we know that if a few guidelines are provided, we will add the essential creative components necessary to create thought-provoking lessons. The new CCSS do not take this away from us. They are standards, they will guide us. But in the end it is the teacher who is the facilitator and knows the needs of the students. We should never lose sight of this.

2. **Educators and parents alike felt that the standards emphasized high-stakes exams and would cause undue stress in students.**

    My Thoughts: The "stress of the test" has been around longer than the CCSS. It is my opinion that other movements in education have more to do with this point rather than the Standards. Educators know that standardized tests are never going away, but, if teachers can find a balance between "Relax it is only a test" and "Let's take this seriously," then our focus remains on a positive classroom environment conducive to learning.

Reasons I Have Embraced the Standards

After I carefully studied the standards, I could see the validity of the objectives and the open-ended nature of the verbiage. I found several positive and innovative ways to look at our curriculum.

1. I feel that the CCSS have actually allowed creativity to be more present in the classrooms. Think about it for a minute. The standards have now become more streamlined in the amount of content we need to teach. This allows more time for the units of study and project-based curriculum that is essential to creativity.
2. "Depth, not just coverage" can be the new mantra in our classrooms; it has been mine for the past 15 years, regardless of a program, mandate, or new educational movement. The CCSS took a buffet of teaching objectives and removed some from our "plates". Because of this, teachers can slow down and focus more on each standard. Do you want to have a choice of thirty objectives or nine standards?
3. I am very excited about the concept of pairing fiction and non-fiction texts and resources in my teaching. Blending genres in all subject areas requires more critical thinking and increases rigor. It (once again I repeat myself a bit) allows time for the creative juices to flow and the varying genres to be recognized. Let me give an example here. Imagine for a moment that I have asked my students to select a fictional chapter book, of their choice, to read. Afterwards I ask for them to look closer at the life of that author and research information about his/her life. Finally I show them how to locate quotes from famous people or song lyrics to help add details about the message of their book. Then, when a summary is written

about their chapter book, my students have some very creative tools that can be used on many formative and summative written assessments.

The world of education is a definite balancing act. Year after year things seem to change. One thing that remains constant to me is that teachers work hard to get vital information and instruction across to their students—learning will take place. I also know that the information in this book can help teachers focus on teaching reading literature, and teach it well and with confidence.

An Overview of the Reading Standards for Literature

I am a pretty simple person and I like my home life and my classroom life to be the same. Too much chaos and my brain becomes overloaded and I become a "Jack of all trades but a master of none." So a couple of years ago I did the best thing for myself and for my students, I slowed down. I know with the onset of the CCSS this notion sounds too simplistic and a little crazy ... but it helped me become a better teacher. I am less stressed, I enjoy my job more and my students are excited to be in class. I do not want anyone to think I am teaching in "Edutopia" because that place does not exist. I am, however, embracing and understanding the CCSS by taking them one at a time. And because I am taking my time to embrace each opportunity the standards have to align my instructional objectives, my teaching has become one of depth and not coverage. And in the end, it is the students in my classroom who are benefiting the most.

When I first looked over the standards I was a touch baffled, even after 24 years of teaching, because of the wealth of information that was coming my way all at once. I barely had time to read the new standards when all of a sudden "the shifts" in ELA were provided to me combined with a mountain of websites of information and to top it off a brand new reading series was presented. I panicked. I could feel my brain going into overload so I took a deep breath and activated my prior knowledge and I slowly began breathe and take one standard for Reading Literature at a time.

One initial method that worked for me was to categorize the standards for Reading Literature. I took one standard at a time and I highlighted the key terms that I knew would turn into my objectives and essential questions. Then I began pulling my existing files and new information I had gathered and started organizing. I rummaged through my supply closet (literally) and found a crate with hanging file folders and went to work. I labeled each folder with the standard number and on sticky notes and notecards I documented all of the key teaching moments that became evident. In the end I had nine folders and nine sticky notes of teachable moments and I started filing. It was a relief to realize that I already had many lessons, ideas, bulletin boards, exit tickets, journal topics, etc. that fit nicely within each folder. I wrote down PowerPoints, websites, reference books that pertained to the teaching standards for each folder on index cards and placed them in the folders as well. I even pulled levelled readers from my reading series that I rarely found time to use and put them in the folders with activity sheets that, again, went with each teachable moment in the folders. When my first crate was somewhat complete, I was ready to teach. I understood that this was an educational journey and that one step at a time would be necessary. After a couple of years using the standards within my units of study, I now have a crate for each study. Start off simple, then watch it grow.

The wonderful thing about this filing and organizational system is that any time I find a great lesson, mentor text, video, etc. that I can use to teach each standard, I have a place to store it. I can't possibly teach everything at once that is available to me and I am not supposed to. When I use an activity or lesson from a standards folder I put it in the back of the folder and when I need to reinforce that standard later on I use a new method that I find in the front of the folder. I also have my computer set up with desktop folders labeled just like the ones in the crate. But instead of housing hard copies, I am collecting online activities, free downloads, and lessons that correlate with my teaching crate. It is a system that continually keeps me organized and helps me understand what I need to teach with regard to the CCSS: Reading Literature.

Teachers are good at differentiating any lesson to meet the needs of the grade-level that they teach. Once I began studying the standards for grades 2–5, the similarities and "spiral curriculum" became evident. I then knew I had a road map ready to plan out my year.

Let's take a closer look at how I labeled my folders and the "notes" I took for each standard. Remember these are focused on the *fourth grade standards* but the word variations of the other grades are very similar. A correlation chart of the standards in grades 2–5 is also available in this chapter. So remember, my steps to designing my curriculum were:

1. Create a file folder for each standard.
2. Take notes and highlight teachable moments that each standard presents (I simply used sticky notes, index cards, and wrote on the front if needed) (Figure 1.1).

3. Search through existing lessons and supplemental materials and begin to fill folders.
4. Refer to the correlation chart to see the similarities of other grade level expectations (Figure 1.2).
5. Eventually, have a separate crate for each unit of study. Each crate is a different color as well. I have additional information on this below.

Figure 1.1 My curriculum crates

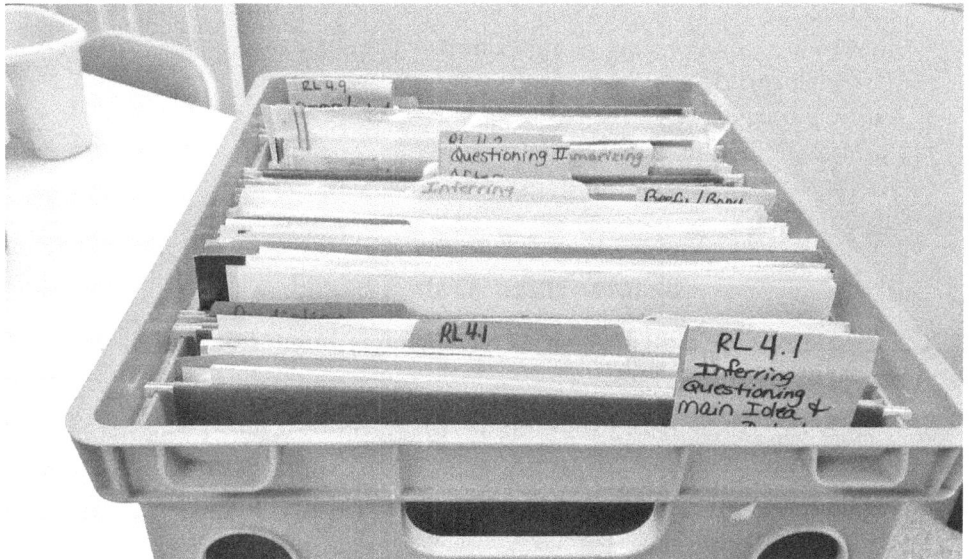

Explaining My Methodology

At the beginning of this journey to understand the standards and create units of study, I tried keeping each standard in isolation, in its own study and its own file in my curriculum crate. But as I became more comfortable, I noticed the overlap of certain goals within the standards. For example, if you look at RL.2, the emphasis is on summarizing and themes. And if you look at RL.9, the emphasis is a deeper study of themes and a comparison and contrast of thematic patterns in literature. So I put them together. In my crate, the RL.4.2 is first and then RL.4.9 follows. The amount of information I have on themes, messages, comparing and contrasting etc. is a crate in itself.

Figure 1.2 A glimpse at my notes

Chapter Two: Crate #1—Blue

RL.4.1—Refer to details and examples in a text when explaining what the text says explicitly and when drawing inferences from the text.

- Details and examples in text (collecting and note-taking while reading)
- Drawing inferences from text (include predictions before reading each day)
- Identify important ideas (determining importance)
- Report ideas either orally or in writing (summarizing, reports, letters of opinion)
- Show evidence in writing using examples from the text
- Main idea and details
- Author's purpose
- Questioning before, during, and after reading
- Questioning: Journalistic and text dependent
- Close reading

Chapter Three: Crate #2—Red

RL.4.2—Determine a theme of a story, drama, or poem from details in the text, summarize the text.

- Identify the problem and solution
- Plot events of the story (sequence)
- Summarize with multiple episodes (several days of reading the same text)
- Remember the story problem when constructing meaning
- Write summaries that reflect literal meaning
- Look closely at themes and messages
- Closer look at details or evidence from the text while summarizing
- Poetry, drama, stories . . . comparing contrasting genres
- Synthesizing
- Retelling vs. Summarizing
- Letters of Comprehension

RL.4.9—Compare and contrast the treatment of similar themes and topics (good/evil) and patterns of events in stories, myths, and traditional literature from different cultures.

- Compare/contrast
- Themes
- Cultural literature

Figure 1.2 *continued*

Chapter Four: Crate #3—White

RL.4.3—Describe a character setting, or event in a story or drama, drawing on specific details in the text (a character's thoughts, words or actions).

- Character attributes/traits
- Character's actions
- Dialectal journals
- Visualizing the setting
- Understanding the relationships among the plot, setting, and character traits (writing to respond)
- Character analysis
- Cause and effect
- Beginning, middle, and end
- Sequencing

Chapter Five: Crate #4—Black

RL.4.4—Determine the meaning of words and phrases as they are used in a text, including those that allude to significant characters found in mythology (Herculean).

- Figurative language
- Descriptive language
- Document details to show character's traits
- Understanding the connotative use of words (own don't rent words)
- Genre-Mythology
- Feelings and sensory awareness
- Word choice
- Vocabulary enrichment
- Visualization
- Genre selections

RL.4.7—Make connections between the text of a story or drama and a visual or oral presentation of the text, identifying where each version reflects specific descriptions and directions in the text.

- Text features (for narrative)
- Visualizing
- Derive information from graphics
- Artistic interpretations

Figure 1.2 *continued*

- Using visual elements to make connections with the text
- Reading aloud for fluency and audience understanding

Chapter Six: Crate #5—Pink

RL.4.5—Explain major differences between poems, prose, and refer to the structural elements of poems (verse, rhythm, meter) and drama (casts of characters, setting, descriptions, dialogue, stage directions) when writing or speaking about a text.

- Making connections to other texts (text to text connections)
- Author study
- Closer look at genres—Poetry and Drama
- Narrative structure vs. other genres (compare/contrast)
- Hybrid texts
- Illustrations

RL.4.6—Compare and contrast the point of view from which different stories are narrated, including the difference between first- and third-person narrations.

- Point of View
- Effectiveness of choice between the 2 "views"
- Writing opportunity—change the point of view of the selection and compare how it effects the reader

Not a Chapter: Crate #6—Green

RL.4.10—By the end of the year, read and comprehend literature including stories, drama, and poetry, in the 4–5 text complexity band proficiency, with scaffolding as needed at the high end of the range.

- Comprehension
- Synthesizing
- Selecting just right books
- Text complexity
- Writing about reading
- Book reports
- Literature circles
- Close reading

* These areas are for the teacher to understand in order to help the students achieve the reading level for CCSS. This is an on-going standard (all of them are) but with more depth and research for the teacher in order to facilitate.

Remember, each box above is a separate crate now and a different color. I did not dedicate a chapter in this book to RL.10 because it is an accumulation of all of the standards and helps with beginning-of-the-year goals and end-of-the-year summative and formative assessments. I do have a stand-alone crate for information on close reading, text complexity, and book reports that are meaningful, etc. Many times teachers will ask me, "Why crates?". I like the portability of them. I can take them home to plan or if I am presenting at my school for a certain unit of study, I can grab and go. Also, if a fellow teacher needs help with finding resources, they are welcome to borrow the crate and make copies. As I said earlier, you can't quite do all of that with a filing cabinet.

Using "I Can" Statements

At the beginning of each chapter, I have included "I can ..." statements. These statements are hung around the classroom during each unit of study. As a self-assessment tool, I give each student a chart for their reading folder that also has these statements written down. As students master the skill, a check is placed beside the statement. There are numerous ways to use these statements. I have also printed each statement on a label. The ink color matches that of the crate color, except for white; I used a grey scale on that label. Each student was given one label at a time, as that particular skill was taught, and it was placed on a page in the reader's notebook. Then students reflected further. Figure 1.3 is an example of an "I can ..." statement from Chapter 3 and how a student responded to the statement.

Figure 1.3 Sample "I can ..." statement and student response

I can write a summary of the information without telling every detail.
RL.2 and RL.9

Student Response:

I learned that there are short summaries and long ones. The 9-1-1 strategy was my favorite way to summarize because it was fun. It also made me focus on what was important. I also learned that retelling is a simple way to remember what I read, but that we don't write those down, they just help us verbally get ready to write a summary.

It Takes a Village

I believe that if teachers will work together to not only study and organize the CCSS, but also share ideas, lesson plans, websites and other valuable information, they have just made their jobs that much easier. As Bill Richardson, the politician, says, *"We cannot accomplish all that we need to do without working together."* Have a "fill the folders" afternoon and invite fellow teachers to bring the pot of coffee while the others can donate the goodies to snack on while the work is being completed. I am always amazed at how, when one teacher shares an idea, it sparks a new idea from someone else and, before you know it, everyone walks away with a wealth of knowledge and a feeling of being part of a team. After our "fill the folders" get together, I was admittedly amazed at how prepared I felt to teach the new Reading Literature standards. My team had fun, worked hard, and walked away with our curriculum crates filled with exciting and innovative teaching tools. One of my favorite quotes about sharing sums up this process of creating a grade-level curriculum crate (Figure 1.4).

Figure 1.4 One of my favorite quotes

> *"If you have an apple and I have an apple and we exchange these apples then you and I will still each have one apple. But if you have an idea and I have an idea and we exchange these ideas, then each of us will have two ideas."*
> George Bernard Shaw

Looking Beyond Your Own Grade Level

One of my main goals for studying the standards and creating my curriculum crates was to feel comfortable with my understanding of, not only what I was expected to teach as in fourth grade, but what the teachers prior to me and after me were also expected to teach. Why is this so important? Because vertical-aligned standards across grade levels encourage a shared responsibility for teachers. It just makes sense for teachers to know where students "have been", where they "are now" and where they "have to go." It helped me to correlate the standards for grades 3–5 and that is when I began noticing and noting the teachable patterns. Table 1.1 is the one I created and still use today. The "teachable moments" column can be added to at any time. Like everything else in my classroom, it is a work in progress.

Table 1.1 Correlation Chart of Standards in Grades 2–5: Reading Literature

GRADE 2	GRADE 3	GRADE 4	GRADE 5	TEACHING MOMENTS/ UNITS OF STUDY
CCSS.ELA—Literacy.RL.2.1 Ask and answer such questions as **who, what, where, when, why, and how** to demonstrate understanding of **key details in a text**.	CCSS.ELA—Literacy.RL.3.1 **Ask and answer questions** to demonstrate understanding of a text, **referring explicitly to the text as the basis for the answers**.	CCSS.ELA—Literacy.RL.4.1 **Refer to details and examples in a text** when explaining what the text says explicitly and when drawing inferences from the text.	CCSS.ELA—Literacy.RL.5.1 **Quote accurately from a text** when explaining what the text says explicitly and when **drawing inferences from the text**.	Questioning Inferring Details/examples in text (CLOSE reading) Main Idea Author's Purpose
CCSS.ELA—Literacy.RL.2.2 **Recount stories**, including fables and folktales from diverse cultures, and determine their central message, lesson, or moral.	CCSS.ELA—Literacy.RL.3.2 **Recount stories**, including fables, folktales, and myths from diverse cultures; determine **the central message, lesson, or moral** and explain how it is conveyed through key details in the text.	CCSS.ELA—Literacy.RL.4.2 **Determine a theme** of a story, drama, or poem from details in the text; **summarize the text**.	CCSS.ELA—Literacy.RL.5.2 **Determine a theme** of a story, drama, or poem from details in the text, including how characters in a story or drama respond to challenges or how the speaker in a poem reflects upon a topic; **summarize the text**.	Themes/message/moral Determining Importance Summarizing/recounting Fables, folktales, myths, poems, stories, and drama
CCSS.ELA—Literacy.RL.2.3 **Describe how characters in a story respond** to major events and challenges.	CCSS.ELA—Literacy.RL.3.3 **Describe characters** in a story (e.g., their traits, **motivations, or feelings**) and explain how their actions contribute to the sequence of events.	CCSS.ELA—Literacy.RL.4.3 Describe in depth a **character, setting, or event** in a story or drama, drawing on specific details in the text (e.g., a **character's thoughts, words, or actions**).	CCSS.ELA—Literacy.RL.5.3 **Compare and contrast two or more characters, settings, or events in a story or drama**, drawing on specific details in the text (e.g., how characters interact).	Character Analysis Compare/contrast of events, characters, settings, themes, etc. Sequence of Events Story Elements Cause/Effect

Table 1.1 continued

GRADE 2	GRADE 3	GRADE 4	GRADE 5	TEACHING MOMENTS/ UNITS OF STUDY
CCSS.ELA—Literacy.RL.2.4 Describe how **words and phrases** (e.g., regular beats, alliteration, rhymes, repeated lines) supply **rhythm and meaning** in a story, poem, or song.	CCSS.ELA—Literacy.RL.3.4 **Determine the meaning of words and phrases** as they are used in a text, distinguishing literal from nonliteral language.	CCSS.ELA—Literacy.RL.4.4 **Determine the meaning of words and phrases** as they are used in a text, including those that allude to significant characters found in mythology (e.g., Herculean).	CCSS.ELA—Literacy.RL.5.4 **Determine the meaning of words and phrases** as they are used in a text, including **figurative language such as metaphors and similes.**	Figurative language Similes/Metaphors Idioms Alliteration Vocabulary * The craft of writing
CCSS.ELA—Literacy.RL.2.5 Describe the **overall structure of a story**, including describing how the beginning introduces the story and the ending concludes the action.	CCSS.ELA—Literacy.RL.3.5 **Refer to parts of stories,** dramas, and poems when writing or speaking about a text, using terms such as **chapter, scene, and stanza;** describe how each successive part builds on earlier sections.	CCSS.ELA—Literacy.RL.4.5 Explain major differences between **poems, drama, and prose,** and **refer to the structural elements of poems** (e.g., verse, rhythm, meter) and drama (e.g., casts of characters, settings, descriptions, dialogue, stage directions) when writing or speaking about a text.	CCSS.ELA—Literacy.RL.5.5 **Explain how a series of chapters, scenes, or stanzas** fits together to provide the overall **structure of a** particular story, drama, or poem.	Text features in stories and poems Sentence fluency Dialogue Brilliant beginnings Mighty middles Excellent endings
CCSS.ELA—Literacy.RL.2.6 Acknowledge differences in the **points of view of characters,** including by speaking in a different voice for each character when reading dialogue aloud.	CCSS.ELA—Literacy.RL.3.6 Distinguish their **own point of view** from that of the narrator or those of the characters.	CCSS.ELA—Literacy.RL.4.6 Compare and contrast the **point of view from which different stories are narrated,** including the difference between first- and third-person narrations.	CCSS.ELA—Literacy.RL.5.6 Describe how a **narrator's or speaker's point of view** influences how events are described.	Point of view First person Third person

CCSS.ELA–Literacy.RL.2.7	CCSS.ELA–Literacy.RL.3.7	CCSS.ELA–Literacy.RL.4.7	CCSS.ELA–Literacy.RL.5.7	
Use information gained from the **illustrations and words in a print or digital text** to demonstrate understanding of its characters, setting, or plot.	Explain how specific aspects of a text's **illustrations contribute to what is conveyed by the words in a story** (e.g., create mood, emphasize aspects of a character or setting).	Make connections between the text of a story or drama and a visual or oral presentation of the text, identifying where each version reflects **specific descriptions** and directions in the text.	Analyze how **visual and multimedia elements** contribute to the meaning, tone, or beauty of a text (e.g., graphic novel, multimedia presentation of fiction, folktale, myth, poem).	Visualization Illustrations Mood/tone Quick sketch Oral presentation
CCSS.ELA–Literacy.RL.2.9	CCSS.ELA–Literacy.RL.3.9	CCSS.ELA–Literacy.RL.4.9	CCSS.ELA–Literacy.RL.5.9	
Compare and contrast two or more versions of the **same story** (e.g., Cinderella stories) by different authors or from different cultures.	Compare and contrast the themes, settings, and plots of **stories written by the same author** about the same or **similar characters** (e.g., in books from a series).	**Compare and contrast** the treatment of **similar themes** and topics (e.g., opposition of good and evil) and patterns of events (e.g., the quest) in stories, myths, and traditional literature from different cultures.	**Compare and contrast stories in the same genre** (e.g., mysteries and adventure stories) on their approaches to **similar themes and topics.**	Compare and contrast Author study Text to text connections Text to world connections Themes

Hard Work Pays Off

Teachers have high expectations of their students as well as themselves. It is in our nature to strive to do the best that we can. At first I was leery of "yet another new program" for education. If you have been teaching as long as I have (or longer), you know that the pendulum swings every 5–7 years. It certainly can be frustrating. I have often wished that everyone would just "make up their minds" and stick to one plan. It seems teachers just get used to one set of standards or program, find that it is working, and then a new one is introduced. But most teachers understand that, even though it can be frustrating, these changes keep us learning. The CCSS filled many educators with dread and fear . . . myself included. But as I began to look at the new standards and at the comprehension strategies and practices that I knew were already set in place, and working, it became obvious for me to just combine the two. It took a little time to organize the standards with my existing information (units, websites, songs, charts, lesson, etc.) but once I worked hard to gather my existing materials and search for new ones, I had a road map that made sense. I want to share this road map with you.

Units of Study: Depth not Coverage

The format of this book is designed to combine the standards that cohesively flow together into units of study for reading literature and comprehension. A unit of study is a set amount of teaching time to focus on similar learning skills. This set amount of time allows teachers to focus on the depth of their teaching and not just a swift coverage of skills. This ideal is one of the reasons I found myself embracing the standards. Teachers use units of study all of the time in writing (narrative, persuasive, poetry, etc.). A teacher could not effectively teach a poetry lesson one day and then a narrative lesson the next and expect students to have time to grasp and master the concepts of the two entirely different writing genres. Instead, teachers set aside 2–3 weeks to focus primarily on poetry and the skills associated with that genre. Then after formative and summative assessment, the decision to continue with poetry or start a new focus on a narrative writing unit of study is made. The basis for teaching reading skills is the same. The studies I have aligned in the following chapters keep teachers and students focused on particular skills that will be built upon and revisited throughout the year. The threads that connect them all are the Common Core State Standards. The units of study within the Reading Literature unit are:

Questions, Inferences, and Purpose (Chapter 2)

  Details, Summaries, and Themes (Chapter 3)

  Character Analysis and Story Elements (Chapter 4)

  Craft and Vocabulary Development (Chapter 5)

  Structural Elements and Point of View (Chapter 6)

I break these units of study into two rotations. The amount of skills necessary to master each component of the study can't possibly be taught just once and never revisited. Here is a sample of my long-term planning.

August:

  Introducing the Reader's Workshop (1–2 weeks)

  Questions, Inferences, and Purpose (1–2 weeks) (Chapter 2)

  Details, Summaries, and Themes (1–2 weeks) (Chapter 3)

September:

  Character Analysis and Story Elements (2 weeks) (Chapter 4)

  Craft and Vocabulary Development (2 weeks) (Chapter 5)

October:

  Structural Elements and Point of View (1–2 weeks) (Chapter 6)

  Comparing and Contrasting with Text Connections (1–2 weeks) (Chapter 6)

This timeframe of studies completes my first 9½ weeks of instruction. Sometimes it may take longer, but never by much. I plan my studies at the beginning of the year using my curriculum crate and a large calendar. I put my "tentative" plans on sticky notes so that they can be manipulated as needed. After this first rotation of my Reading Literature curriculum, I am ready to introduce a Reading Informational Text curriculum that in itself is broken down into smaller units of manageable studies. That typically takes me through January, and then I repeat my Reading Literature curriculum. Remember you will have so many ideas, lessons, etc. in your curriculum crate that revisiting Reading Literature will not feel like you have to start "all over" again. Plus, since the first rotation focuses on depth, not coverage, students remember the previously taught information and are ready for new objectives and layers of skills to be introduced. I can usually cut in half the time for my second rotation, so I am looking at 4–5 weeks for my new rotation. That gives me 4–5 more weeks of Reading Informational Texts before the state mandated tests roll around in the spring.

Let's look at an entire year long-range plan. Please note that teachers must be flexible and not use any long-range plan as a "cookie-cutter" model. Also remember that I take roughly 2 weeks at the beginning of the school year to go over rituals and routines and set up my reading workshop. This is why the first rotation of my Reading Literature curriculum seems a little longer.

August–October: Reading Literature (Tying in genres)

November–January: Reading Informational Texts

February–March: Reading Literature (Tying in genres)

March–April: Reading Informational Texts

Content Area Reading

I am responsible for teaching the ELA block to my fourth grade students. I team teach with another teacher who teaches the science, math, and social studies curriculum. In the content subjects of science and social studies, the students are reading informational texts on a daily basis with my teaching partner. Because of this, I am very comfortable with focusing on reading literature first and then switching to informational texts the way that the long-range plan shows. While we are working on the Reading Literature unit, my students are engrossed in literature texts during independent reading. When I shift to the informational text unit, students are reading informational chapter books, trade books, etc. during the independent reading time. My writing instruction also correlates. Whatever genre we are focusing on, we are also learning to write that particular genre as well. For example, I focus on personal narratives, fables, myths, legends, and poetry while working through the first rotation of a Reading Literature unit of study. Then in February when my second rotation begins, I focus on the genres of fictional narratives, plays, reader's theaters, tall tales, and mysteries. I focus on expository and persuasive writing while working in the informational text unit of study. All the while, my students are also reading and writing in the content areas of science and social studies, but with my teaching partner.

Resources for Teachers

Teachers can never have enough information at their fingertips. It keeps our teaching fresh and interesting not only to our students, but also to ourselves. The curriculum crate can help organize all of this information. The following resources are tried and true. I have them in my "favorites" folder on my computer. I have some of the lessons and ideas from these sources printed out and placed in my own curriculum crate. The first listings of websites are not just about CCSS or about reading instruction. They are filled with educational activities, lesson plans, and articles that can easily be added to the curriculum crate that was described in this chapter. Following the general resources, I have provided a listing of websites, blogs, and professional books that are specific to the common core.

Websites

- www.abcteach.com
- www.apples4theteacher.com
- www.edhelper.com
- www.educationworld.com
- www.learningpage.com
- www.lessonplanspage.com
- www.pbs.org/teachers
- www.schoolexpress.com
- www.teachernet.com
- www.ed.gov
- www.writingfix.com
- www.readworks.org

Common Core Resources

Websites

- commoncore.org
- ccsstoolbox.com
- literacydesigncollaborative.org

- teachingchannel.org
- achievethecore.org
- commoncoreinstitute.org

Blogs for CCSS

- blog.commoncore.org
- commoncoretools.me
- blog.coreknowledge.org
- commoncorefacts.blogspot.com
- allthingscommoncore.com

Professional Books on CCSS

- *Understanding the Common Core State Standards*
  by John S. Kendall
- *The Core Six: Essential Strategies for Achieving Excellence with the Common Core*
  by Matthew J. Perini
- *Using the Common Core Standards to Enhance Classroom Instruction and Assessment*
  by Robert J. Marzano
- *Better Learning Through Structured Teaching*
  by Nancy Frey
- *Aligning Your Curriculum to the Common Core Standards*
  by Joe T. Crawford
- *Non-Fiction Strategies that Work: Do This—Not That*
  by Lori G. Wilfong

Choice Boards

At the end of each chapter, before my closing thoughts, I include a choice board for a culminating review of the standard(s) covered in that chapter. Each choice board can be used as a class wrap-up, station work, homework, or practice during independent reading. The choice boards can also be used as a formative or summative assessment and have written response opportunities as well. The possibilities of curricular options are numerous.

Closing Thoughts

I am an eternal optimist. More importantly, I believe in teachers. I see what they do and I know the road to teaching is difficult and arduous. I have walked the walk. So many times I will pick out a professional teaching book only to find that the author is not or has not been a classroom teacher, or I will read an article that is politically etched in facts that are not conducive to what teachers truly face each day. My goal, my one simplistic goal, is to make the lives of teachers easier and more manageable. By working together to create curriculum crates or by investing a little time for a professional book study, or even better yet, just being there to positively tell each other that "we can do this", the collaboration and support that all teachers need can be achieved. Statistics show that almost 50 percent of teachers leave the profession after only 5 years. It doesn't have to be this way. Look, the CCSS are here for a while. Who knows for how long. But instead of letting ourselves get stressed or confused, or overloaded, why not slow down a bit. Go get the crate and the file folders, gather up your grade-level colleagues and let's take a closer look at just how to meet the standards for Reading Literature . . . one unit of study at a time.

Chapter 2

Questioning, Inferring, and Author's Purpose: A Likely Trio for Comprehension

"Once you learn to read, you will be forever free."
Frederick Douglass

Standard RL.1

I Can Statements

- I can use the details and examples in the text to explain or infer meaning.
- I can define inference and explain how a reader uses details and examples from a text for logical conclusions.
- I can read closely and find answers explicitly in the text.
- I can read closely and find answers that require an inference.
- I can analyze an author's words and refer to details and examples needed to support both explicit and inferential questions.
- I can infer the author's purpose using clues from the text.

Figure 2.1 Another look at my notes

Chapter 2: Crate #1—Blue

RL.4.1. Refer to details and examples in a text when explaining what the text says explicitly and when drawing inferences from the text.

- Details and examples in text (collecting and note-taking while reading)
- Drawing inferences from text (include predictions before reading each day)
- Identify important ideas (determining importance)
- Report ideas either orally or in writing (summarizing, reports, letters of opinion)
- Show evidence in writing using examples from the text
- Main idea and details
- Author's purpose
- Questioning before, during, and after reading
- Questioning: journalistic and text dependent
- Close reading

Questioning and Inferring—Intertwining the Two

As I looked closely at the two comprehension strategies, questioning and inferring, I began to envision how these two strategies could intertwine together into a unit of study. I found that they fit nicely together because:

1. When students read for comprehension, they ask questions in their minds about what they are reading. Students must ask questions and seek answers to deepen their understanding of the text before, during, and after reading. In other words, students are thinking through internal questioning while they are reading.

2. When students "read between the lines" and recognize and gather all of the clues that the author has given them in the story, they are making meaning of the text through inferring (before, during, and after reading). When inferring, students are using their background knowledge to make predictions as well as to draw conclusions from the implied information in their reading. Many critics of the CCSS insist that background knowledge is no longer taught and that it needs to be. I agree that background knowledge is important to

comprehension, but I am confused when I hear that it is not an evident skill in the CCSS. If you look closely at the verbiage in RL.4.1 and RL.5.1, drawing inferences is part of the standards. The definition of inferring is for readers to think about and search the text, and sometimes use *personal knowledge to construct meaning beyond what is literally stated.* I have always considered the author's purpose to be inferred, because unless the author walks into our classroom and discusses with us why the piece was written, we are making an educated guess. That is one reason why this unit of study includes author's purpose.

3. Once students have asked internal and external questions, sought out the answers to these questions, as well as combined what they know from background information or clues provided by the text, they can draw conclusions, or summarize the text. These summaries are based on text evidence found in the reading material. Chapter 3 looks closely at summarizing as well as story elements.

Starting from the Beginning

As I begin to focus on one area of comprehension at a time I understand that comprehension is not an isolated set of skills, but rather a blending of them all. But I also understand that introducing strategies in more manageable "chunks" helps me plan efficiently and ensures that my students grasp the concepts. I enjoy building my curriculum spirally. I am constantly adding to and reviewing the foundational strategies that I begin the year with. In this case, I began my year with a unit of study around the skills of questioning and inferring, (with a dose of author's purpose throughout the year.) My ultimate goal for my students is for them to understand what they read, but also with that understanding lies a well-written summary of important events, details, and evidence from the text or texts. Chapter 3 will cover ways for students to collect information and summarize.

The next sections of this chapter will be broken down into those two units of study: questioning and inferring. I will also include different ways to introduce and teach about the author's purpose.

Quality Questioning

Students have been asking questions and seeking answers since what seems like the beginning of "educational time." Typically the teacher would ask the question, the students found the answers and all was good. Research has taught us, however, that deeper questioning, not just surface questions, helps students relate to the text they are reading as well as understand and take ownership of the information in the text. As Josef Albers, a German artist and educator, stated, "Good teaching is more of a giving of right questions than a giving of right answers." With the CCSS, the teacher begins to step aside as the primary "questioner" and releases that responsibility to the students. The students begin to ask the questions and record their thoughts, findings and answers in journals, reader's notebooks, exit tickets and other writing opportunities. The correlation chart below in Table 2.1 shows how each grade level builds upon the previous one with the level of expectations and understanding increasing with each year.

Breaking Down the Verbiage

I want to take a moment to look a little closer at the information from standard 1. I find that when I break down the verbiage of the standards, I discover the skills waiting to be taught. I do want to stress, however, that my main goal is to teach. Yes "unpacking" the standard is important, creating a curriculum is important, but so is enjoying what you do. Sometimes teachers, myself included, lose sight of the reason we went into teaching. To help students discover who they are and the possibilities that await them in the future. My goal when I walk into my classroom each day is *not*:

1. To have lesson plans that are very lengthy and took hours away from my teaching or grading time.
2. To become so wrapped up in the language of the standards that the breathing and living element (the students) in the classroom are overlooked.
3. To become stressed over the new requirements of CCSS because after looking closer at the standards and breaking down the requirements, I see that the curriculum is manageable.

So now that we can all take a sigh of relief, let's look at standard 1 and break down the components (Table 2.1).

In second grade, we can see that the "journalistic questions" are introduced. The basic "who, what, where, when, why, and how" have been asked for years. It is important for students to recognize these types of questions in their reading. In second grade, the answers to these questions can be recorded in reading notebooks or graphic organizers. It allows a quick reference of important details. It is important to note one key word in the

Table 2.1 Standard 1

CCSS.ELA–LITERACY.RL.2.1	CCSS.ELA–LITERACY.RL.3.1	CCSS.ELA–LITERACY.RL.4.1	CCSS.ELA–LITERACY.RL.5.1
Ask and answer such questions as who, what, where, when, why, and how to demonstrate understanding of key details in a text.	Ask and answer questions to demonstrate understanding of a text, referring explicitly to the text as the basis for the answers.	Refer to details and examples in a text when explaining what the text says explicitly and when drawing inferences from the text.	Quote accurately from a text when explaining what the text says explicitly and when drawing inferences from the text.

* Please note that the word "predicting" is not in the CCSS; however, that does not mean that students will not make predictions. This is the entry-level skill before inference is taught. Relating to one's background knowledge is a natural element in problem-solving and constructing meaning.

standard: "*ask*". With CCSS the students are not simply answering these journalistic questions on a worksheet, they are asking themselves these questions while reading. What is also critical is that students need to recognize when the answers to these questions surface during their reading. This is why a reader's notebook or a graphic organizer is an important tool to provide to students so that while their brains begin asking the questions during reading, they have a place to capture the questions as well as the answers. Another important part of the standard to notice is the requirement for details from the text to be provided. I call it proof or evidence. Sally may write down that the setting is in a forest (the *where* journalistic question) but I need her to also document the details and descriptive words the text offers about the setting. In other words, I want her to prove to me that the setting is in the forest but also recognize the descriptive words that add to visualization of the forest. The T-chart below (Table 2.2) can be created in a graphic organizer or students can simply draw it in their reader's notebooks. It can be used during independent, small-, or whole-group reading. I advise that teachers model how to use this chart on many occasions during a read-aloud, to ensure that the students understand the process of collecting the information.

For grades 3–5, the use of a T-chart is also an excellent tool to provide to students. It is the difference in the language of these T-charts that sets them apart based on the standards. Let me take a second here to let you

Table 2.2 Levels of Questioning

JOURNALISTIC QUESTIONS: W5 + H1	DETAILS FROM THE TEXT
Book Title:	
Who (Characters in the story)	
What (What are the major events—the plot)	
Where (Where does the story take place—the setting)	
When (When does the story take place—past, present, future)	
Why (Why is the main character having a problem)	
How (How is the problem solved or how does the story end)	

know that I use all of the charts with my fourth graders. I want to review the journalistic questions as well as text evidence, quotes, and inferences. It is a spiral curriculum and each grade level reviews older standards as well as introducing future standards. I tend to use the journalistic question at the beginning of the year as a review and then concentrate on questions during reading before the focus changes to the details and quotes that the standards from the fourth and fifth grades address. The importance of *evidence from the text* when answering questions is apparent from day one and it is the common thread in this set of standards. See the variations in Tables 2.3–2.5.

Table 2.3 Third Grade T-chart

QUESTIONS DURING READING	ANSWERS WITH EVIDENCE FROM THE TEXT

Table 2.4 Fourth Grade T-chart

IMPORTANT DETAILS AND EXAMPLES FROM THE TEXT	MY THOUGHTS, INFERENCES AND QUESTIONS

Codes: T—thoughts. I—inferences. Q—questions

Table 2.5 Fifth Grade T-chart

QUOTES/EVIDENCE FROM THE TEXT	MY THOUGHTS, INFERENCES, AND QUESTIONS

Codes: T—thoughts. I—inferences. Q—questions

Generic Organizers for Responding to Reading

Looking closely at the standards and creating tools that align with the objectives of the standards, as in the T-charts, is only one way to help our students recall information, ask questions, look at evidence, etc. The following organizers can be used throughout any mini-lesson or unit of study. Some of the verbiage may be tweaked to meet the purposes of the lesson, but these are tried and true ways to help your students collect information and thoughts while reading as well as prepare for summarization.

Table 2.6 Responding to Questions

QUESTION TYPE	MY QUESTIONS	SPARKED BY SOMETHING I READ ON PAGE . . .
Asking about the basic facts		
Wondering about predictions		
Why or how		
Wondering about connections		
Thinking about my feelings		

Descriptions with Evidence

Directions: Based on your reading of (fill in title here) _____, describe three events, characters, or changes in the chart below. Support each of your descriptions with evidence from the text.

Table 2.7 Sample Chart

THREE _____ (EVENTS, CHARACTERS, OR CHANGES)	EVIDENCE FROM THE TEXT
1.	1.
2.	2.
3.	3.

* An easy way to summarize a piece of reading is to look closely at characters, events, and major changes that have taken place. After several days of reading I ask my students to write a 3-paragraph summary: one paragraph for the characters, one for the events, and one for the noted changes in the book.

Table 2.8 KWL Chart

KNOW	WONDER	LEARNED

Coding Questions

There are many levels of questioning. To help my students "see" the differences in the levels, I bring in a few manipulatives and some questioning stems. I bring in a bag of bolts, nuts, and screws for the "robot", a magnifying glass for the "detective", a gavel for the judge, and a beaker for the inventor. I have also been known to wear dark glasses, a trench coat and a hat for the detective and of course a white lab coat for the inventor. The chart below is an example of these four levels of questioning.

Figure 2.2 Levels of questioning

Robot

- Who is . . . ?
- What is . . . ?
- Where is . . . ?
- When is . . . ?

Questions regarding characters, setting, and problem

Detective

- Why is . . . ?
- What caused . . . ?
- How is . . . ?

Judge

- Who would . . . ?
- Who might . . . ?
- Where could . . . ?
- Do you agree . . . ?
- In your opinion . . . ?

Inventor

- Why would . . . ?
- How would . . . ?
- How might . . . ?
- What would you . . . ?
- What would happen if . . . ?

Flip-it

Flip-it is a strategy for answering questions that involves restating the question. This simple, yet effective, strategy helps ensure that students will focus on the purpose of the question and the evidence from the text to answer the question. It is basically a restating strategy. When we play this game in the classroom, I have index cards with a question written on each one. A student selects a card, reads the question aloud and then "flips it" in order to practice answering the question using the language from the question. The full answer does not have to be stated, just how the question would be answered. Now, if the class is reviewing a story that was read in class, then students would complete the full answers. If the strategy of restating a question is simply being reviewed, then just the statement is needed. The answer is on the back of the index card and the student "flips it" as well to check himself. Here is an example:

Figure 2.3 Front of card

> Why did Travis feel his role in the family was to be a provider?

Figure 2.4 Back of card

> Travis felt that his role in the family was to be a provider because . . . (Students can stop here if it is a restating review or provide the complete answer if it is a review about a story read in class.)

Asking Questions

Students asking questions before, during, and after reading to enhance interest and comprehension is an important strategy for them to use. Students are natural-born question askers and often teachers are bombarded with many questions throughout the day. But students also need to realize that asking questions internally while they are reading is a key component of comprehension. This opportunity for questioning is not explicitly noted in the CCSS, but as teachers we understand that it is implicitly suggested. It is a natural teaching moment to discuss and question a topic or a mentor text, etc. Many teachers wonder if, because of the lack of verbiage in the standards, the *before questioning* that builds on background knowledge should be introduced. My thoughts are, how could it not? To engage students in a dialogue about something they are about to read can clarify their thinking and help you find out what they already know or expect from the material. Questions and discussion also clarify understanding during and after reading. One way to begin this dialogue is through asking questions that elicit responses reflecting the students' thoughts and understandings about the reading.

Too often, questions are used only at the end of reading, asked by the teacher or tutor to check comprehension. In fact, successful readers ask themselves questions throughout the reading process. Beginning readers need modeling and practice to learn how to do this.

Effective questions encourage real thinking, not just yes or no answers. Notice too that different kinds of questions require different ways of finding the answer:

- **Factual or "right there"** questions can be answered with a single word or phrase found right in the story: "When did the story take place?" "It was midnight, the 25th of October . . . " These are completely evidence-based type questions. The students can "touch the text" to find the answers. One of the major shifts in the CCSS was text-based evidence.

- **Inference or "think and search"** questions require finding and integrating information from several places in the story and relating one's own knowledge as well. "When did the story take place?" "The harvest moon hung high in the sky, shining on the field of ripe orange pumpkins waiting to be picked for Halloween . . . " Using our background knowledge of concepts such as "harvest" and "Halloween" as well as the words "ripe pumpkins" we figure out that this story takes place one night in late October, even though those words aren't used in the text. The CCSS are reliant on drawing inferences from the text and explaining explicitly what the text says.

- **"In the head" or "on my own"** questions require bringing in one's own information (background knowledge). These can be answered without reading from the book. "We have read a lot of fairy tales, what kinds of things usually happen in fairy tales?" Or, "You told me you have a cat. What might happen in a story called Puss in Boots? Do you think it could be true?" While the questions that adhere towards background knowledge are not explicitly written within the CCSS, the cue words "to demonstrate understanding of a text" support the necessity of these types of questions. Teachers may not ask students to focus on their background knowledge as much, but I know that, in my classroom, I see it as an effective tool for connecting with the text.

Questions before reading should help the reader:

- **Make connections** between background knowledge and the topic of the book: "This book is about Anansi the Spider: Do you remember the other Anansi book we read? What kind of character is Anansi? What kinds of things did he do in that story? How do you suppose he will behave in this book?"
- **Set a purpose** for reading: "Here is a new book about sea turtles. What are some things that you would like to learn about these creatures?"
- **Make predictions**: "The title of this book is *The Missing Tooth* (Cole, 1988). Who do you suppose the two boys on the cover are, and what do you think this book might be about? What happens to you when you lose a tooth?"

Questions during reading should help the reader:

- **Clarify and review** what has happened so far: "What are some of the things that made Arlo and Robby such good friends?"
- **Confirm or create new predictions**: "Now that one boy has lost a tooth, so they aren't both the same, what's going to happen? I wonder if they will stay friends."
- **Critically evaluate the story and make personal connections**: "Could this really happen—that two good friends could have a fight because one of them had something the other wanted? How would you feel if you were Robby? What would you do?"
- **Make connections with other experiences or books**: "Does this remind you of another story/character? What happened in that story? Could that happen here?"
- **Monitor the child's reading for meaning and accuracy**: "Did that word 'horned' make sense? What is a 'horned toad'?"

Questions after reading will help:

- **Reinforce the concept** that reading is for understanding the meaning of the text, and making connections: "In this story about Amy's first day in school how did she feel before going into her classroom? How did you feel on your first day?"
- **Model ways of thinking** through and organizing the information they have taken in from reading a text: "What did Amy's teacher do when she walked into the classroom? How does Amy feel now? How do you know that?"
- **Encourage critical thinking** and personal response: "What do you think might have happened if the teacher had not done that? Why do you think the author decided to write this story? Would you have done what Amy did?"
- **Build awareness** of common themes and structures in literature: "What other story or character does this sound like? What parts are the same? What parts are different?"

When children respond to your questions it is important to listen carefully to what they say, and to respond to any questions they may have. Also, if a student has misunderstood a section of a story, you may want to go back to that part of the book and reread it, clarifying any difficult vocabulary if necessary, to help the student understand what is going on.

You might say:

"You said that the rabbit was laughing at the pig at the end, but you know, I remember something different. Let's look at that part of the book again and see what it says."

(Then reread the appropriate segment of the book.)

"Here it says: 'The rabbit ran through the door and slipped past the man who was laughing at the pig.' Do you know what it means when someone 'slips past' something?"

The most important thing, however, when talking about a story with a child is to let them know that their ideas about what they have read are important and that you value what they have to say.

Mentor Texts for Questioning

Mentor texts are often the missing link between teacher instruction and student understanding. I love books and I love teaching with them. The following list contains examples of mentor texts that I use during a "questioning" unit of study. These books offer the chance for students to dig deeper into their own lives, their own thoughts, and their own wonderings.

- *Fly Away Home* by Eve Bunting
- *An Angel for Solomon Singer* by Cynthia Rylant
- *The Stranger* by Chris Van Allsburg
- *Baseball Saved Us* by Ken Mochizuki
- *Charlie Anderson* by Barbara Abercrombie
- *The Van Gogh Café* by Cynthia Rylant
- *Weslandia* by Paul Fleischman
- *The Name Jar* by Yangsook Choi
- *Everybody Needs a Rock* by Byrd Baylor

Three Ways to Ask Questions

Among the many higher level thinking skills that students need is the skill of generating quality questions. The three activities below are an excellent way for students to become used to being the "questioner" not just the "responder."

1. Asking the Teacher Questions

Teachers know students love to ask us questions, so I devised a way for them to do just that. I print out labels with my name and school address and attach them to basic white (inexpensive) letter-sized envelopes. During independent reading, I ask my students to jot down questions they have about what they are reading. I tell them that this helps me "see inside their minds." This activity also works well in a literature circle, but is just as effective when students have various self-selected texts. It is also an excellent way for students to interact after the daily read-aloud. As the students read and record their questions on sticky notes, index cards, strips of paper, etc. they place the questions in the envelope. At the end of the week I take up the questions and read through them. This is an excellent formative assessment activity. It immediately lets me see who understands the process of asking deeper complex questions and those who are strictly asking the generic journalistic style questions.

Examples:

1. In Chapter Three, why did _____ decide to _____?
2. Do you think _____ will become friends with _____? Why?
3. What was your favorite part of Chapter Three?
4. How do you think the problem will be solved?
5. What is the setting of the story?

I keep an anchor chart handy and we categorize the questions I have had "mailed" to me. Each chart represents a level of questioning:

Figure 2.5 Sample chart

"Right there" questions:

* Who, What, Where, When?

Figure 2.6 Sample chart

"Think and search" questions:

* Why ...? What caused ...? What happened first, second, or third? What are the characteristics of ...? Character/Setting/Problem/Solution/Events

Figure 2.7 Sample chart

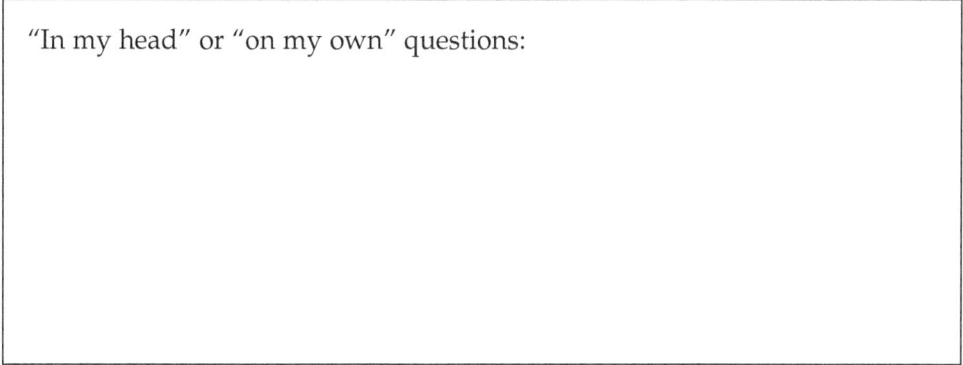

* Do you think ...? How would you ...? Which is better ...? Would you agree ...? Were you ever ...? In your opinion ...?

2. Asking the Author Questions

Once students become comfortable asking the teacher questions, it is time to "bump up" the activity just a bit and ask the author questions. This type of questioning allows the students to become more connected to what they are reading and even become more connected to the author. These types of questions engage students in the reading and help solidify their understanding of the text. It also helps students "critique" the author's writing. That is also very helpful during writing instruction as well. Exactly how do students question the author? To introduce this strategy, teachers need to select a short passage or several pages from the read-aloud that day. Then the teacher models through the questioning. Some examples might be:

- What is the author trying to say?
- Why do I think the author used the following phrase?
- I wonder why the author picked this title for the story.
- What does this author seem to think is so important?
- At this point I think the author wants us to think ....
- What can you infer about the author's feelings in this section of the text?

Author Studies

To add a higher level of interest, merge an author study within the questioning and inferring unit of study. For example, I love Patricia Polacco, she is my writing guru, who I can always trust. I simply use her books during an author study each day for my read-aloud, tying in the skills necessary for questioning and inferring. Then, at the end of the study, I have students research about her life and we use this information in a biographical piece of writing. Students have also summarized the unit by writing letters to Ms. Polacco and addressing some of the questions they had while they were "questioning the author". A quick Internet search will reveal the addresses and contact information of most popular authors. You can really feel the excitement buzzing in the classroom when an author we wrote to writes back to us!

3. Asking Other Students Questions

It's quiz time! And this time the students are the ones that do most of the work. This activity is fun, creative, and beneficial. I typically introduce this strategy during a read-aloud. The students are sitting up front and close to me ... with their reader's notebooks in hand. As I read, they begin to jot down questions based on the text. These questions are more along the lines of the "right there" style of questioning. In other words, the answers can be touched and proven. After the book has been read, I ask students to select their favorite generated question. These questions are written on index cards and placed in a bucket. Then it becomes a review tool. While students are reading independently, I look through the bucket of questions as a formative assessment. If I see a question that is confusing, I conference with the student who wrote the question and get clarification. If I see a repetitive question, I simply ask for one of the students to select a different one from their reader's notebook. After independent reading, the students come back to the front and I pull out the questions one by one and they are answered.

Going Deeper Within the Study

The second layer of this unit of study is inferring. It is almost impossible to look at making inferences without first looking at making predictions. And even though the verbiage is not explicitly used in the CCSS, teachers realize the "close cousins" are too similar and important to neglect introducing as they get into the study.

What is a Prediction?

Figure 2.8 Making predictions

> *"Research suggests that when students make predictions their understanding increases and they are more interested in the reading material."*
> Fielding, Anderson, Pearson and Hanson

A prediction is simply what you think will happen based upon the text, the author, and your background knowledge. In other words it is an educated guess as to what will happen. When students make predictions, typically the predictions will be answered by the end of the story or chapter. The reader focuses on what will happen in the story. Readers can make predictions before, during, and after reading. But making predictions involves more than just trying to figure out what happened in the story. As students find "evidence" to form predictions they are also:

- asking questions
- recalling facts
- skimming and scanning the text
- inferring
- drawing conclusions
- ultimately comprehending the text more fully.

I ask my students to predict, in their reader's notebooks, what they think might happen in the chapter of the book they are reading during independent reading time that day. Then after the reading session has ended, the students reflect back on their predictions to see which ones were correct. A simple table like the one in Table 2.9 is a great way for students to organize their predictions and responses.

I will use the same chart to show an example using the book, *Thank You Mr. Falker* by Patricia Polacco (Table 2.10). I model this strategy for collecting evidence and making predictions several times using picture books. Then, when I see that the concept has been grasped, the students begin to model the same process during their independent reading time.

As the year progresses, I add an additional column for *revision* to the chart (Table 2.11). The revising column is a place for students to recognize

Table 2.9

CLUES/TEXT EVIDENCE	PREDICTION	CONFIRMATION

Table 2.10

CLUES/TEXT EVIDENCE	PREDICTION	CONFIRMATION
Trisha began to feel different. She began to feel dumb.	She is going to begin to dislike school.	True
When Mr. Falker discovers her secret, he sets out to help her prove she can read.	Mr. Falker is going to be the one to help her.	True

Table 2.11

CLUES/TEXT EVIDENCE	PREDICTION	CONFIRMATION	REVISION

the prediction was incorrect so a new prediction is created or the original prediction is slightly adjusted, or revised.

I often provide students with mini-anchor charts that are glued into their reader's notebooks. The chart in Figure 2.9 is a simple "reminder" of what a prediction is. I also provide any type of graphic organizer, text excerpt, etc. to add to the notebooks. These charts add to or enhance my reading mini-lesson for the day. I find that if a standard graphic organizer is shrunk to 85 percent, it will fit nicely into a reader's (or writer's) notebook.

Figure 2.9 Mini-anchor chart about predictions

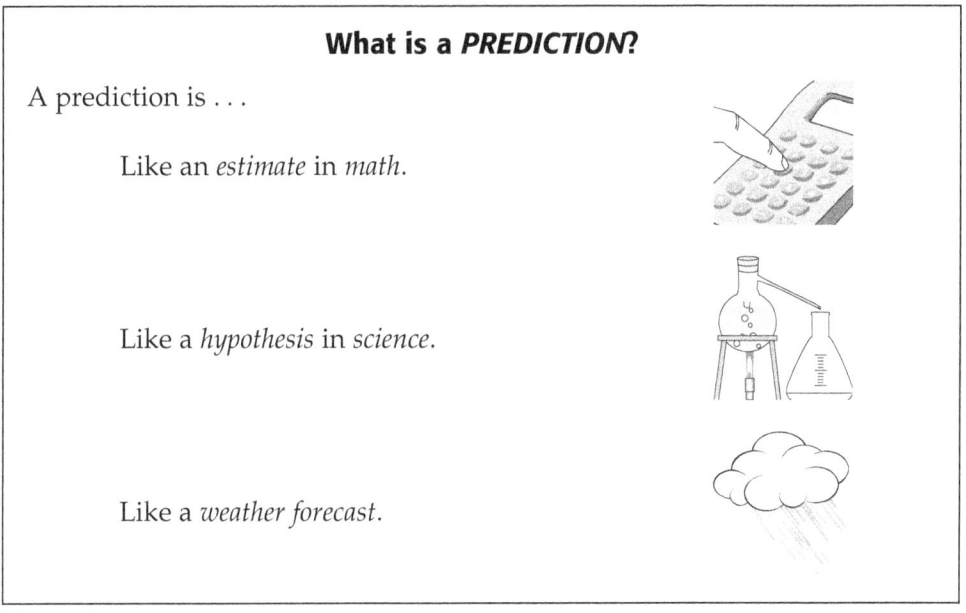

Books are one of the core tools in a classroom, and teaching mini-lessons with them is even better. One of my favorite quotes I came across in my reading is, "Books are not the icing on the cake, they are the cake." I cannot imagine introducing the day's lesson without first modeling the skill (or the task at hand for the day) with a well-loved mentor text. Remember mentor texts are not just books. They can be poems, articles, excerpts from a favorite chapter book, a recipe card, or sales catalogue item description. The more teachers vary the types of mentor texts they use, the better.

Mentor Texts for Predicting

- *Aunt Harriet's Underground Railroad* by Faith Ringgold
- *Cinder Edna* by Ellen Jackson
- *Class Clown* by Robert Munsch
- *Good Night Moon* by Margaret Wise Brown
- *The Island of Skog* by Steven Kellogg
- *Grandfather Twilight* by Ralph Fletcher
- *The Sign Painter* by Allen Say
- *Alexander and the Terrible, Horrible, Very Bad Day* by Judith Viorst
- *City Green* by Dyanne DiSalvo-Ryan
- *Duck for President* by Doreen Cronin
- *Fly Away Home* by Eve Bunting
- *Zeke Pippin* by William Steig
- *Dory Story* by Jerry Pallotta
- *Never Ever Shout in the Zoo* by Karma Wilson
- *Stephanie's Ponytail* by Robert Munsch

Making Predictions from the Blurb

Students are making predictions throughout the day, even when book browsing. Showing students how to use the book blurb is an excellent way for students to select a "just right" book to read that grabs their attention. The mini-anchor chart in Figure 2.10 is introduced to the students, then modeled using a stack of chapter books I have selected. Finally, it is glued into the reader's notebooks and used for selecting a book to read during independent reading time.

What is an Inference?

An inference is an intersection of meaning. Students take clues from the text plus their background knowledge (schema) to form an inference. Inferences help readers because they make them connect what they are reading to the information that they already know. In order to draw conclusions and evaluate a text, students must rely on circumstantial evidence and prior

Figure 2.10   Mini-anchor chart sample

What Can We Learn From the Blurb?

- The main character
- The problem/issue
- The setting
- Hints of the resolution
- The big idea, lesson, or message of the story
- The topic or theme
- The genre

Figure 2.11   What is inferring?

> *"Inferring is at the intersection of taking what is known, garnering clues from the text, and thinking ahead to make a judgment, discern a theme, or speculate what is to come."*
>
> Harvey and Goudvis

knowledge. This strategy is often referred to as "reading between the lines." While the CCSS presses teachers and students to focus heavily on text-based evidence, answering inference questions asks students to go beyond immediately available information. I met a teacher at one of my workshops that had pre-cut pieces of fake "fur" and when one of her students answered an inference question (for example, "What type of person was Goldilocks?") she handed them a little square of the fabric that they kept on their desk for the remainder of the day. Then that student's name was added to a bulletin board with the title, "We Like to In-Fur!" Anything to make teaching exciting, right? Students also connect with the following discussion stem that I use to introduce inferring. I like for everyone to be sitting close together at the front and I write the following question on the board. "Has anyone ever tried to tell you something without coming right out and saying it?" I give them a moment to read the question and think. Then I might say something along the lines of, "If so, you had to infer what he or she was telling you. Who would like to share when this has happened to you?" It doesn't take long for students to start talking and giving examples, and I am also awarded the opportunity to get to know a little bit more about them. I find that I just need to stop sometimes and let the students talk and, in this case, it is tying right in with what we are studying.

Text-based Inferences

Table 2.12 is an example that I use to help students organize their thoughts while reading. The students make a simple T-chart and label one side with "When the text said . . . " and the other side with "I can INFER . . ." I stress

Table 2.12 Text Inferences

WHEN THE TEXT SAID . . .	I CAN INFER . . .
My mother hid my little sister and me under the bed.	* She doesn't want them to get harmed by the soldiers. * The girls are probably frightened.
"I must have your wedding ring", my father told my mother.	* They didn't have enough money.
Her face twisted the way it did when she closed the door of our home for the last time.	* Mother was scared and worried.
I saw him look at my mother across our heads.	* The father was trying to be strong and not scare them.
Everyone was quiet and my mother gripped my hand.	* She is trying to give hope. * She was trying to be courageous.
I was afraid to hope.	* She didn't want to get her hopes up and be disappointed.

* A summary can easily be written that focuses strictly on the inferences made through text examples during a designated amount of time reading. I like to ask my students to summarize after a week of "taking notes" using one of the many graphic organizers found in this chapter.

the use of text evidence when students are making an inference. If they are reading a chapter book, I ask that the page number where the evidence was found be included.

Layering the Instruction

There are several important concepts that will be taught during the inferring layer of the study. I have included a mentor text for each concept that can be used as an introduction.

1. Inferring with wordless books. *Hiccup* by Mercer Mayer
2. Inferring with picture books. *Encounter* by Jane Yolen
3. Inferring by making predictions. *Legend of the Indian Paintbrush* by Tomie DePaola
4. Inferring with text without illustrations. *Slower than the Rest* by Cynthia Rylant
5. Inferring with poems. *Compass* by Georgia Heard
6. Inferring about characters. *Babushka's Doll* by Patricia Polacco
7. Inferring about theme. *Fables* by Arnold Label
8. Inferring about unfamiliar words. *Piggens* by Jane Yolen
9. Inferring to answer questions. *Five Dollars* by Jane Little
10. Inferring based on a dramatic action. (Act out situations)
11. Inferring about the author's purpose. (I used the iguana theme)

    - To persuade: *I Wanna Iguana* by Karen Kaufman Orloff
    - To entertain: *Private I. Guana* by Nina Laden
    - To inform: *Iguanas!* by Becky Wolf

Thinking Stems for Inferring

These stems can be posted on an anchor chart or jotted down in a reader's notebook for easy reference (see Figure 2.12).

Figure 2.12 Sample thinking stems

My guess is . . .

Maybe . . .

This could mean . . .

Perhaps . . .

I predict . . .

It could be that . . .

Quick Inference Activities

Got a few minutes? Try some of these activities as either a review or introduction to making inferences.

- **Play Charades**
  Students find a section of their independent reading books (or in the basal story if you use those) where evidence of emotions and action are taking place. Students take turns reading this selection out loud making sure to add voice and gestures. The other students infer opinions about the character based on the charade.

- **Comic Strips**
  Students can fill in empty comic strip bubbles. The students infer what the characters are saying to each other by the setting, the facial expressions, etc. I simply white-out what is in the bubbles and make copies. Then I show the original comic after everyone has filled in their own, and we compare.

- **Guess What**
  Show students an unfamiliar object and allow them to make inferences about what the objects may be. I like to use pictures (or actual ones if handy) of antique tools.

- **Headlines**
  Share newspaper headlines with students and let them infer what the article will be about. An example of a headline that I have used before is *Miners Refuse to Work after Death.*

- **Dialogue Detective**
  During your read-aloud, model for students where you found a section of dialogue that taught you a lot about the characters who are conversing. Write this conversation in speech bubbles in your own reader's notebook. Then have students do the same thing with their independent reading books.

- **Actions Speak Loudly**
  Each day, during my read-aloud, I show students how I take notes about the characters. As I come across a character in the book, I jot his or her name down. Then when that character acts in a certain way, I take note of it. For example, when I was reading *Old Teller*, by Fred Gibson, aloud to my students, I came to the part when Travis had to make the gut-wrenching decision to "shoot his old yeller dog." Beside Travis' name, in my notebook, I wrote "courageous and loyal". Then I put the page number that proved his actions and supported my inference about his character.

- **Name that Inference**
  For this activity, students are given an index card with a situation written on it. The card is read aloud and the other students take guesses at naming the inference. Figure 2.13 shows a few of the "situations" I write on the cards.

Figure 2.13   Sample situations

- The ride was quite enjoyable. Our hair blew in the cool autumn air as we rounded each curve of the mountain. (riding in a convertible)
- Darkness was all around us. The only available light was from the flicker of the candle that was set on the mantle. The rumbling was getting closer. (a storm is coming and the power went out)
- I told my dad to slow down, but he continued to race along the interstate. He was in a hurry to get to the soccer game. All of a sudden we saw blue lights. (speeding ticket)

Inferring with Poetry, Pictures, and Wordless Books

Poetry

I love poetry. I believe that poems should be used as often as possible in instruction. In my classroom, we have sections of our reader's notebooks that house all of the poems that we use throughout the year. I have, in the past, had a separate notebook just for poetry, and that worked as well.

When students make an inference about a poem, I provide everyone with a copy of the poem. I read the poem aloud first and then call on volunteers to read it as well. I also like having poetry partners, where two students sit close together and practice reading the poem to one another. These poetry partners are also useful when students need to discuss the author's purpose, their thinking during the poem and any inferences that were made. Poetry is also an excellent tool to use for teaching visualization, fluency practice, close reads, connections, vocabulary, you name it. I have often wondered why some teachers shy away from using poems in the classroom. I don't mean teaching a large unit on reading and writing poetry, which I also recommend, but simply having a poem a week that students read, glue into their notebooks, and learn from.

The organizer below (Figure 2.14) shows how students can glue a poem onto one side of the paper and respond on the other. Because we use the reader's notebooks so much, I find that I do not make many copies of organizers; my students can just paste the poem into their notebooks and reflect on it out to the side. You will see that the poem below is almost like a riddle. It gives "hints" along the way at what the object might be. Of course, we know it is a stapler, and the students will make that guess pretty easily as well. It is the *evidence* and clues within the poem that we stop and notice in order to come to our conclusion, or rather our inference. An additional lesson to piggyback this one is to let students write their own object poems and let the other students make guesses.

Figure 2.14   Organizer for poem and response

POEM	My Thinking/Evidence Noticed
With tiny teeth	
of tin	
they take	
one slender	
breath before they make	
a move,	
and then,	
a silver pinch!	
with jaws	
no bigger	
than an inch	
these dragon grips	I'm inferring
are small and slight-	
but	
conquer pages	
with	
one	
bite!	

52 • Questioning, Inferring, Author's Purpose

Students can make inferences, not only about the subject of a poem, but also the mood, the author's purpose, and the setting. Let's take a "conversational look" at a haiku poem and break down the process of inferring.

Poem Examples and Inference Questions

Me: We have been learning about making inferences for the past week or so. When you make an inference with a poem, it may be more difficult at first because poets typically try to say a great deal with little words. We are going to look closely at the following poem. It is a haiku, and remember that a haiku has a syllable count of 5-7-5. In the following lines of a haiku poem "Miserable Afternoon", your job will be to infer the setting of the poem. Let's start by carefully reading the poem. And let's not forget that the title holds some clues as well.

> Crystals fall from trees
> Wandering around numbers
> Headstones tell little

Questions to Help Make Inferences

Me: Ok, now that we have read and reread the poem it is time to infer the setting. To help you figure out the setting of the poem, you first need to know what a setting is. You might already know that the setting usually deals with time and place.

It is sometimes easier to make an inference when questions are generated. Let's brainstorm some possible questions that we have:

The students generate questions, with my guidance, and I write them down on an anchor chart.

Me: What a great job you did with asking questions. Let's reread those questions together.
1. What time is it?
2. What are crystals falling from the trees? Could it be a reference to the weather or water?
3. What is a headstone? Where do you find headstones? What would headstones tell or reveal?

4. What does the author mean about numbers? What is significant about numbers? Why are there numbers in a cemetery?

Now I want you to take a few minutes and investigate and ask yourself the questions we just generated together. Jot down any answers and inferred thoughts in your reader's notebooks.

At this point, I give students time to reflect. Here are some of the answers to the questions I received. I wrote these answers out beside the questions on the anchor chart.

Billy: The title of the poem tells that it is a "Miserable Afternoon." This is not really making an inference, but this is a clue to part of the setting. The time of day is afternoon.

Bella: Crystals could be a reference to snow or ice. So, you could infer that it is probably wintertime.

Annalie: Headstones are found in a cemetery. So, you can infer that the poem probably takes place in a cemetery. A headstone tells who is buried there. It is usually a stone marker that stands the test of time. But I still don't know where the cemetery is.

Me: What do the numbers have to do with a cemetery? If you do a little research, you will find that cemeteries that have grave markers or headstones with only numbers are sometimes found beside hospitals or institutions in years past. It was less costly to place a number on a stone instead of whole names and additional information.

Inference Answer

Me: With all of this information that you have found with your inference investigation you might have come up with the following answer for the haiku poem "Miserable Afternoon."

The setting of the poem is a winter afternoon in a cemetery by a hospital or institution. The specific time period or year of the setting of the poem is not clear. It could be in the past or the present. Poetry can be easier to understand and figure out if you know the right strategies and investigate using clues.

Additional Resources for Poetry

There are many excellent teacher resources available to teachers that offer poems and suggestions for creative ways to use them in the curriculum. Some of my favorites are listed below. Figure 2.15 shows mentor texts I use for poetry.

- *Teaching Poetry, Yes You Can!* by Jaqueline Sweeney
- *Partner Poems for Building Fluency* by Bobbi Katz
- *Poetry Works!* by Baba Bell Hajdusiewicz

Mentor Texts for Poetry

Figure 2.15   Mentor texts for poetry

Gathering the Sun byAlma Ada

Touch the Poem byArnold Adoff

Laughing Tomatoes by Francisco Alarcon

Nathaniel Talking by Eloise Greenfield

Honey, I Love by Eloise Greenfield

Falling Down the Page by Georgia Heard

Creatures of the Earth, Sea and Sky by Georgia Heard

The Dream Keeper by Langston Hughes

Once I Ate a Pie by Patricia MacLachlan

Sky Scrape/City Scrape by Jane Yolen

* Any books by Jack Prelutsky and Shel Silverstein

The Power of Pictures

A picture is worth a thousand words, or one good inference. I always keep a large collection of pictures I find in magazines or catalogues. I also add postcards to the mix. Students enjoy bringing in samples to add to our class picture file as well. It is a great way to spark an interest in what is happening in class. In the back of our reader's notebooks a sandwich baggie is taped to the back inside cover and students keep pictures inside the baggie that they can use, not only in reading, but also in writing. A collection of pictures can help to teach external character traits, setting, dialogue, and of course inferences. As with poetry, these are a must in the classroom. To teach inference I distribute pictures from the picture file. Each picture has a number on the back of it. It is easier to start with pictures of people that are found in magazines or catalogues. The expressions on their faces are the evidence we are looking for in order to make an inference. I like to break up the students into groups of around 4–5. Each student studies their picture and jots down the number on the back, as well as what details they see. Is the person smiling? Do they look irritated? Or maybe crying? Then students look within the background of the picture and try to determine, through an inference, why this person is exhibiting the emotion (facial expression) that they are. The next step is for students to exchange pictures with another student in their group. It is simpler if students sit in a circle and pass the pictures clockwise. It gets a little less confusing for the younger grades. Teachers know that sometimes group work can cause some logistical issues, so I try to think of possible problems that might occur and "nip those in the bud" before the activity even starts. The clockwise rotation works every time. We often chant, "To the right . . . to the right!" After a few minutes of observing their new picture, each student writes down the picture number on the back, and again makes an inference of the emotion and the cause found within the evidence in the picture. After a few more exchanges, students share and compare. It is always interesting to listen in on the conversations about why each student came to the conclusion they did. There are two professional books that I recommend for teachers to add to their library, *Write What You Know* by Hank Kellner and *101 Picture Prompts to Spark Super Writing* by Karen Kellaher. Even though these books are geared towards writing instruction, the pictures are inspiring and intriguing enough to use for teaching multiple comprehension strategies, such as inferring.

Inferring with Wordless Picture Books

There are many ways to teach with wordless (or nearly wordless) picture books. One of my favorite ways is for making inferences. Students form groups of two to three and grab a stack of sticky notes and pencils. Then together the students look at the book they have selected, study the illustrations and can do one of two things:

1. Create a text for each page, that goes along with the pictures
2. Ask inferential type questions or statements based on the pictures

    "I wonder why the boy looks so sad?"

    "It looks like a storm is coming!"

There are many excellent mentor texts available, and each year more and more titles are published. The power of pictures is evident. Figure 2.16 shows a few of the titles I keep in my wordless book basket.

Figure 2.16 Titles in my wordless book basket

Deep in the Forest by Brinton Turkle

10 Minutes till Bedtime by Peggy Rathmann

Looking Down by Steve Jenkins

Carl's Summer Vacation by Alexandra Day

Tuesday by David Wiesner

Chicken and Cat by Sara Varon

Do You Want to Be My Friend by Eric Carle

The Snowman by Raymond Briggs

Anno's Counting Book by Mitsumasa Anno

Zoom and *Re-Zoom* by Istvan Banyai

Inferring vs. Predicting

Predicting is a type of "forward inferring", whereas other inferring happens while looking back, or at the present moment of reading. Although predicting and inferring overlap, inferring is more difficult because readers must be more precise. Predicting is something you can check for accuracy by further reading and adjusting, if necessary. Inferring, however, is not as easy to get feedback on. In other words, an inference is a well-supported thought through text evidence, clues, and background knowledge, and looks closely at the *present* and the *past*. A prediction is made on text evidence and not much else and looks closer at the *future*.

Predicting and Inferring Bookmarks

I love teaching with bookmarks, and my students enjoy using them. I often laminate a class set of bookmarks that students use during that unit of study. In this case, I have the predicting bookmark on one side and the inferring bookmark glued on the other side (Figure 2.17). These bookmarks are laminated and ready for students to refer to during their independent reading time.

Figure 2.17 Predicting and inferring bookmarks

Predicting	Inferring Bookmark
* A prediction is a good guess about what the story will be about or what might happen next.	TEXT + ME = INFERENCE
	* When you use clues from the text and your own schema, you are inferring.
Make a prediction when . . .	
• You read the title	**Sentence starters**
• You see a heading	• This makes me think of . . .
• The author asks a question	• This makes me think that . . .
• You have a good idea about the story	• At first I thought . . . but now I think . . .
• A chapter ends	• This clue leads me to believe . . .
• You begin a new chapter	• After reading this page/chapter, I think I understand what the author's meant when he or she wrote . . .
* You should always have a reason for a prediction. Good readers make a prediction many times during a story.	
	• If I were the main character I would . . .
• Based on the title (or pictures), I predict that this story will be about . . .	• The author didn't say this but I know . . .
• I think the next chapter (or page) will be about . . .	• I think the main character is a _____ person because . . .
• Based on (a clue), I predict . . .	• I think the author's purpose for writing this is . . .
• Based on what _____ (a character) said or did, I predict . . .	

A Closer Look at Author's Purpose

As stated earlier, I look at author's purpose as more of an inferring skill. As students become more familiar with the purposes, I "stretch out" the basic PIE acronym to PIEES. The author's purpose in reading can be to persuade, inform, explain, entertain, or show emotions.

Figure 2.18 PIEES anchor chart

P is for PERSUADE

I is for INFORM

E is for EXPLAIN

E is also for ENTERTAIN

S is for SHOWS EMOTIONS

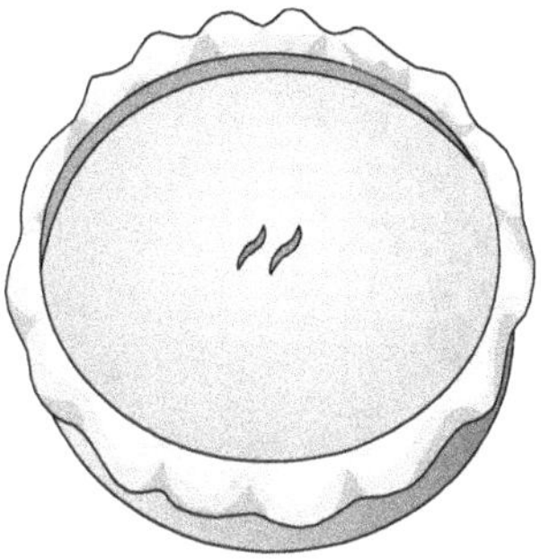

Keeping a Running Record

Author's purpose is one of those skills that is constantly reinforced. At the beginning of the year, when students are first looking closely at the author's purpose, I stick to the basic PIE (persuade, inform, and entertain) acronym that has been used in classrooms for years. Each time I read a book we discuss why the author more than likely wrote the piece. I also make sure that my students understand that sometimes there may be a combination of several purposes within one text. One way to record the types of purposes that have been recognized in class is to create a large Y symbol on chart paper. Label each section with a P-I-E. The goal of the chart is to record titles and ask ourselves "Why did the author write this?" (see an example in Figure 2.19).

Figure 2.19 Chart example

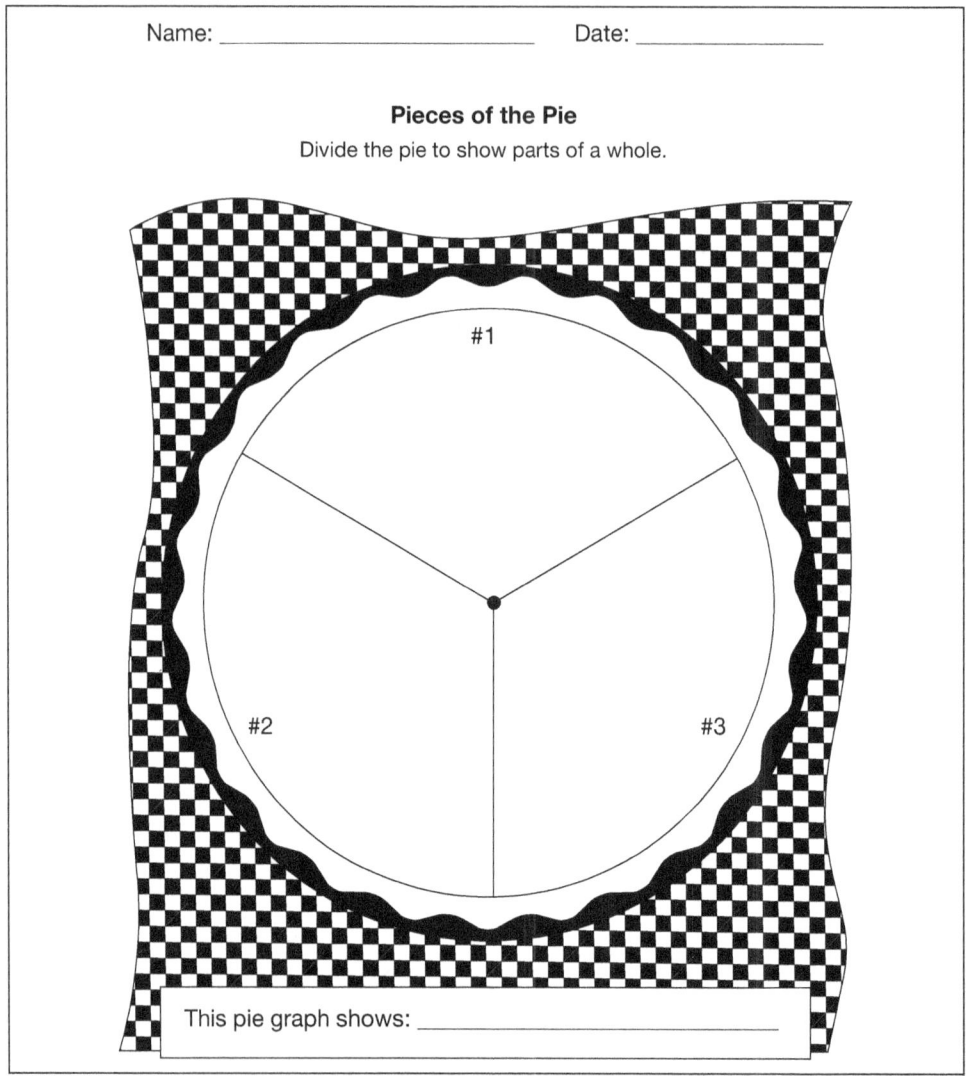

60 • Questioning, Inferring, Author's Purpose

Figure 2.20 Student example

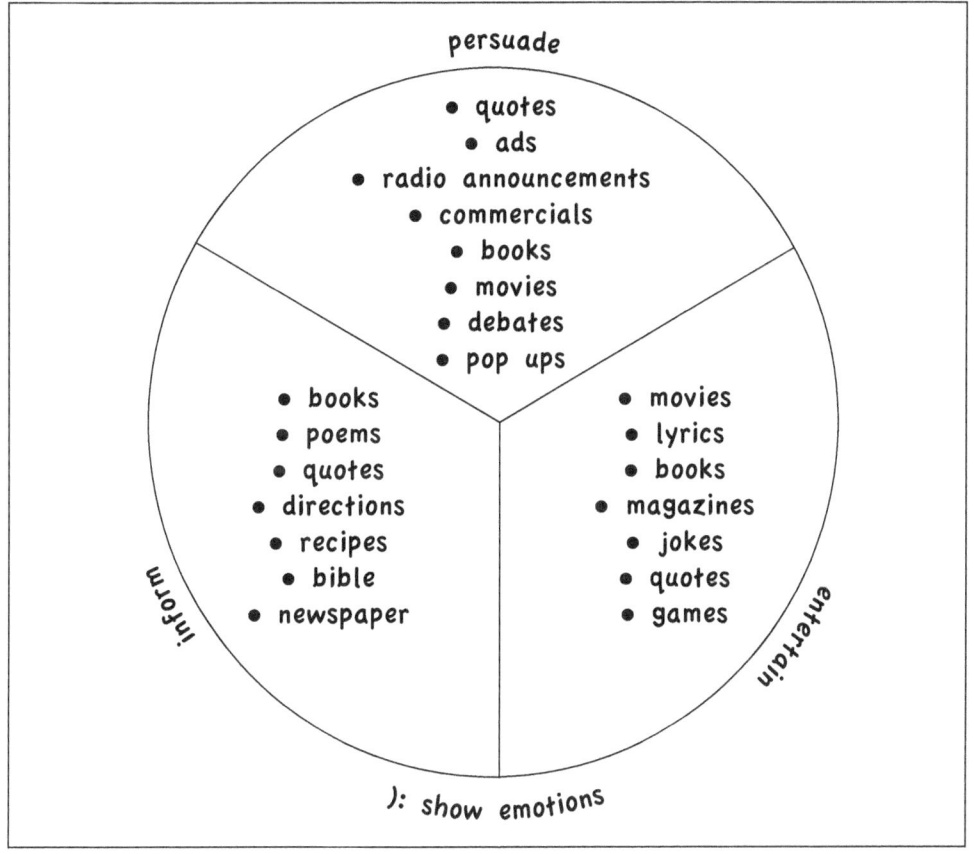

Questioning, Inferring, Author's Purpose ◆ 61

Choice Board

R	E	A	D
Look at the front cover and reread the title of a book that you have not read yet. What can you infer about the book just by the title?	Read the blurb on the back cover of a book that you have not read yet. What can you infer about the book just from the blurb?	Write at least three inferences that you can make about a character based on his/her actions or thoughts?	Choose one piece of character dialogue. What can you infer from this dialogue?
Write three statements about the book you are reading following this format: I can infer . . . because the text says . . .	Create four questions using who, what, where, why, or how. Then answer the questions using details from the story.	Think about the setting of the story. What can you infer about the setting based on the details in the text to support your description?	What can you infer is the author's purpose for writing the story? Use evidence and explicit details from the text to support your inference.

Closing Thoughts

Deeper thinking is one of the keys to comprehension. I know that if my students are not rereading, reflecting, and asking questions then real reading is not taking place. By hovering over the comprehension strategies of questioning and inferring, teachers are showing students what real readers do. And when we tie in the author's purpose, we are layering the instruction of inferring as well as connecting with who wrote the text.

Chapter 3

Guiding Students to Write Sensational Summaries and Recognize Themes

"The more that you read, the more things you will know. The more you learn the more places you will go."

Dr. Seuss

Standards RL.2 and RL.9

I Can Statements

- I can determine the main idea of what I read and explain to my teacher or a peer using details from the text.
- I can create a summary of the information without telling every detail.
- I can analyze details in a text to determine a theme I can define in summary.
- I can write a summary using details from the text.
- I can discuss how themes and events are similar from one story to another. I can define a theme.
- I can identify similar themes, topics, and patterns of events found in stories, myths, and traditional literature from different cultures.

Figure 3.1 Another look at my notes

Chapter 3: Crate #2—Red

RL.4.2: Determine a theme of a story, drama, or poem from details in the text, summarize the text.

- Identify the problem and solution
- Summarize with multiple episodes (several days of reading the same text)
- Remember the story problem when constructing meaning
- Write summaries that reflect literal meaning
- Look closely at themes and messages
- Closer look at details or evidence from the text while summarizing
- Poetry, drama, stories . . . comparing contrasting genres
- Synthesizing
- Retelling vs. Summarizing
- Letters of Comprehension

RL.4.9: Compare and contrast the treatment of similar themes and topics (good/evil) and patterns of events in stories, myths, and traditional literature from different cultures.

- Compare/contrast
- Themes
- Cultural literature

The Importance of Summarizing

It seems so simple. Read and write a summary. Students are asked to extract the important events from a story, poem, article, etc. This strategy demands students to determine what is important by stripping away the redundant and extraneous samples. So how do teachers get students to "get to the point" and "look closely at details?" Simple anchor charts (I use large chart paper) to record student responses to the following questions break down the responsibility of writing a summary:

- What is summarizing?
- Why do readers summarize?
- How do readers summarize?
- When do readers summarize?

In this chapter, you will find several suggestions for summarizing. I find that if I can give my students a goal for their daily reading, the more efficient and intent the reading becomes. And when I model what I am looking for with my daily read-aloud as well as provide a place (graphic organizer, reader's notebook, etc.) for students to collect and salvage their thoughts, writing detail and evidence-based summaries is not so difficult anymore.

Before we take a closer look at the teachable moments of standards 2 and 9, let's look at the differences between two major terms these standards focus on: *recount* and *summarize*. In grades 2–3 the word *recount* is used for checking understanding. The definition of "recount" is to tell someone about something; to give an account of an event or experience. In other words, to retell in detail. A few synonyms for *recount* are:

describe

retell

relate

narrate.

In grades 4 and 5, the use of the word *summarize* is evident. The definition for "summarize" is to give a brief or descriptive statement of the main points, important facts and critical details of something. Some synonyms for *summarize* are:

abridge

condense

write a synopsis

"put in a nutshell."

Why Use Summarizing in the Classroom?

1. Summarizing is a key reading strategy. If a student can't summarize, chances are that complete comprehension did not occur.
2. Summarizing requires a reader to think about what was read and recall important events.
3. Many standardized tests or county "cold reads" require students to write summaries.

What Makes a Good Summary?

A summary should include the following:

1. names of important characters and settings;
2. important events of the story, in sequential order;
3. a sentence or two about the underlying theme or message of the story.

A good summary should not include the reader's opinion or trivial details. Later in this chapter, distinguishing what is important from what is interesting (or trivial) is looked at closer. Teachers can help students learn to summarize by beginning with retelling and, also, taking a few moments to create an anchor chart that answers the question, "What makes a good summary?". Begin with the three areas listed above and let students elaborate from there.

Summarizing vs. Retelling

Retelling and summarizing are two important strategies for reading. Retelling is a verbal opportunity to reflect on what was read for the day. For example, after reading a story, a reader retells the story by putting it into his or her own words. Even though retelling and summarizing are similar, it is important to consider the differences when planning classroom instruction.

Why Use Retelling in the Classroom?

Retelling is a powerful tool for building comprehension. Because it is not typically written, it is an excellent way to begin this unit of study on summarizing. Students are more comfortable when they talk first and write later. Retelling about a fictional piece also requires students to think about the characters, setting, conflict, and important events. This all becomes very important when teachers layer the curriculum with a written response.

How Do We Use Retelling in the Classroom?

The simplest way to use retelling is with a partner reading of the same text or short story. Teachers may even use the weekly basal story. Later on, students can retell about what they are independently reading, even if their partner is in a different chapter book. My students love it when we use the retelling ropes for this skill.

The retelling rope is exactly that. I bring in several pieces of rope and I tie four knots in each one. After I have read a book, I call on a student to retell the story I have just read, at the same time touching each knot of the rope. Each knot represents a character, setting, problem or solution. After we have practiced this as a class during several read-alouds, it is time for partners to pair up. Each pair of students has a rope, with four knots, to retell events of their story to their partner.

Determining Importance

When I first began teaching, the philosophy was "more is better." We now know that this is not necessarily the case. In the earlier grades the word recount is used because it allows students to restate (retell) the material without being centrally concerned about the length of the writing. The skill of recounting (retelling) is more concerned with restating material differently than the original version. The evidence from the text is still important but there is wiggle room for personal connections.

In grades 4 and 5, however, the term "summarize" is introduced and the length of writing does become an important factor. This is where teaching students how to determine what the most important details are falls into play. This is the time to use the backpack analogy below because the purpose of the summary is to condense source material into a *shorter form*.

Thinking within the Text: The Backpack Analogy

The importance of text evidence, details, and examples is obvious in most of the Reading Literature standards. But careful selection of this evidence is a lesson in itself. When I am packing for a trip, I usually challenge myself to only take one suitcase. I am not sure why a woman would want to do this, but it is a game I have played for years. I must be very selective and only pack the most important items. I use this example with my students with regard to determining what is important within a text that they are reading or one they are listening to. "We can't highlight or jot down everything." I gently remind my students. And in the case of the suitcase, "We can't pack it all!" To provide a visual for my students I bring in a small backpack. I explain that my big suitcase is packed and that I am allowed a small carry-on that must be small enough to fit under the seat of the plane or in the storage compartment above the seat in the airplane. The following conversation shows how this role-playing defines determining importance to my students:

> *OK students, I am excited to tell you that I have won the grand prize in the writing contest that I entered. I am travelling to Ireland for a week and need some help packing this small backpack. The airlines are very picky about the size and weight of the bag. So we must determine what the most important items for me to take are. My larger suitcase with my clothes and other personal items will be checked in at the airport. I won't have access to that bag until after the plane has landed. This small backpack needs to be filled with important items that I may need during the plane ride. Remember, sometimes airlines can lose your luggage so I want to be prepared if this happens. Here are the items we need to choose from.*

I actually received a "packing list" from an online vacation website. I printed this out to show my students. It also helped me think of items that I could bring in to "pack". Anyone can find a handy must-pack type list on the Internet. All of the items on the list do not have to be brought in, but I can project the list and continue to role-play or I can bring several of the items on the list into my classroom ... or I can do a little of both. In this case I actually brought all of the items in.

On a side-note, these packing lists can be photocopied for students and used in a writing piece where students can only select five items to bring on a trip and they must explain *why* they chose the items they did. I have also asked my students to write a carry-on baggage advice column. This required students to research and take notes from several sources they found on the Internet. The possibilities are endless, but all tie into one strategy: determine importance. And once students can do this, their summaries are more concise. Let's continue with the conversational journey:

> *Class, I want to show you a handy must-pack list that I found on the Internet. I brought in many of the items so you can help me determine what is important to pack in this small case. Here is the list of items:*

>   sunblock   comfortable shoes
>   electrical adapters   translation guide*
>   toothbrush/toothpaste   snacks
>   first-aid kit   wash kit (soap, shampoo,
>   umbrella/poncho   razor, etc.)
>   hat   itinerary/tickets*
>   sunglasses/prescription   pen and paper
>   glasses   foreign currency*

sewing kit/safety pins
small flashlight
chargers/cell phone
tourist guide*
hand sanitizer
important documents (passport,
   ID, travel insurance)*
deodorant
change of clothes
books, magazines
list of important phone numbers
camera
cash, credit cards, travelers
   checks*
insect repellent

It is important to note that there are several vocabulary instruction opportunities to review or introduce to students with this activity. Many of my students do not travel much, so words such as itinerary, poncho, passport, currency etc. can be reviewed during the "packing process". I even bring in a scale and tell the students ahead of time that the weight limit for the stowing compartment on the airplane is 5 pounds and it must all fit neatly in my backpack.

On another note, for the items I cannot bring in an example of, or choose not to bring in, such as the items with the * symbol, I simply make copies of these from an online image or an Internet source.

OK students, let's get busy packing. Let's look at this list and see what I need to pack. Look carefully at each item and determine its importance. Also keep in mind that I may be without my large suitcase for quite a while, and if the airline misplaces my luggage, I must survive for a few days with what is in this backpack. Also keep in mind that I will be in a foreign country.

The conversation continues and, as students suggest an item for me to pack, the reasons why I need this item and the importance of this item are also discussed. After a consensus is reached, I place that item in the backpack. This process continues until my bag is packed.

Determining importance in order to prepare for a summary is a difficult skill for many readers because actually stopping, thinking, and choosing what the most important parts of a story are is a higher level skill that requires lots of modeling. When it comes time to ask students to actually write about these important details found in their text and support their writing with evidence from the book, teachers have now layered the curriculum and, without careful planning and teaching, even the best thought-out efforts can fall short. Since I started using the backpack analogy, I have seen this skill become much easier for my students.

Summarizing to Evaluate Comprehension

Throughout this book, I introduce additional strategies for summarizing. Each chapter will show curricular opportunities for students to summarize their reading. Summarizing is a formative type of assessment that allows teachers to evaluate for understanding and depth of knowledge from their students. I am going to offer ideas and lessons that could be taught in a 1–2 week time frame (that is typically how long my units of study take). However, since teachers need a multitude of lessons and strategies for teaching and revisiting each comprehension skill, each chapter of this book will provide many possibilities. Here are a few that are tried, true, and always a hit with my students.

1. Reactions to the Story

Directions:
Choose five events from the story. Describe each event, then describe your reaction to each event. (Examples: How did it make you feel? Does it create new predictions or change old predictions? Did it surprise you or change how you feel about a character? Did any questions arise?)

EVENT	PERSONAL REACTIONS
1.	1.
2.	2.
3.	3.
4.	4.
5.	5.

* By connecting to one's book selection, through personal reactions, students are paying close attention to what is important. After several days of reading, I have my students write a brief summary using the information that has been gathered. I can use this same organizer all the way through a chapter book as well.

2. Retelling Map

TITLE		
Beginning	Characters	Setting
Middle	Characters	Setting
End	Characters	Setting

* The beginning, middle, and ending tracking page helps students "see" the rising and falling action of what they are reading. After the story (or chapter book) is completely read, a summary describing the B-M-E of the story is ready to be written, and important information is easily recalled.

3. Tracking My Thinking through the Chapters

Book title _____		
Author _____		
Describe important events, characters, and settings in each box. Or attach note-taking post-its to the correct chapter number. Remember your sticky notes can be layered.		
Chapter 1	Chapter 2	Chapter 3
Chapter 4	Chapter 5	Chapter 6
Chapter 7	Chapter 8	Chapter 9
Chapter 10	Chapter 11	Chapter 12

* This is an effective way to see what students are thinking during each daily read while in independent reading time. I like my students to use sticky notes because they can be stacked upon each other when needed. These sticky notes are used to recall events when a summary is written.

4. Tracking Important Ideas/Details

IMPORTANT IDEAS	DETAILS
Page #_____	
Page #_____	
Page #_____	
Page #_____	

* A brief summary can be written about the major events and details of several days of writing by using the "note-taking" tracking activity above. These can be collected and used again when students are asked to write a summary after finishing the book completely.

5. Tracking Changes in My Thinking

My thinking before reading . . .
My thinking after reading some of the text . . .
My thinking changed because . . .
My thinking after reading some more . . .
My thinking changed because . . .

* A summary can be written, after several days of reading, noting the changes in events as well as the thinking of the reader.

6. Storyboard Sketching

> **Directions:**
> In each box, quick sketch one important part of the story. Remember to add details to your drawings.

* A summary can be written about the main events of a story by using the pictures drawn during the daily independent reading time. I ask my students to include details within each quick sketch. These details become important when writing about the main events.

Write Summaries and Recognize Themes • 75

7. Snap a Photo

Directions:

Imagine you are taking a photo of an important event in the story. Show your photograph below. Think about the following as you snap your photo:

1. Which characters are in the photo?
2. What setting is in the background of the photo?
3. What important events are happening in the photo?

---

* This activity can be used after each chapter of a book that the students are reading during independent reading time. A summary of important events can be written using a collection of these "photos."

8. Coding the Reading

One of my favorite ways to really "see inside the minds" of my students is through a coding system. This engages students with a purpose for reading. I often tell my students that if thoughts and questions are not going through their head while reading, then they are not truly reading. As a matter of fact, discussing the importance of recognizing when that "internal thought process" isn't working, and that readers need to realize it and go back and reread, is a major mini-lesson at the beginning of the year. Providing a few sample thinking stems before focusing on using codes during reading is always a good idea to help students recognize their thoughts while reading. I like to color code the thinking stems using different colored sticky notes. It helps students keep track of where their thoughts lie during independent reading. The colors I use are listed beside each stem.

What am I thinking? (pink)

I'm wondering . . . (blue)

I'm noticing . . . (yellow)

I'm thinking . . . (white)

I'm remembering . . . (green)

I'm questioning . . . (orange)

When I can see the thinking processes of my students though thinking stems, I introduce how to code their reading. These two strategies form a natural progression.

When I start the year, I introduce a few codes at a time and then add to the anchor chart as the year progresses. This coding can be done in the page margins, on sticky notes, bookmarks, or in a reader's notebook. As always, demonstrating the skill several times using a read-aloud helps ensure success when students begin to code their own reading. I always make sure that the code of *questioning* is one of the first ones to be introduced. Here are the codes that I use:

!	I agree
✗	I disagree
?	I have questions
❤	I really like this
★	I think this is important
NI	New information I learned

P/S Problem and solution

C Connections

V New or higher level vocabulary

I Interesting part

A Answer to a question

💬 A part that makes me predict or infer

9. The 9-1-1 Phone Call

When teachers ask students to begin telling or writing about what a reading passage or story is about, it is not uncommon for them to start rattling off all of the little details. This simple, fun, and effective strategy is popular with my students. After each day's independent reading session, I ask for the students to come back to their seats, open their reader's notebook to the 9–1–1 page that they have designated and set my timer. I allow 10 seconds (sometimes a little more) for students to write down a quick summary of the day's reading. They understand that only the most important events need to be documented. The sharing of these "phone calls" is the best part. We make a telephone ringing sound, and then one student at a time shares their daily summary. I love how the students act as if they were really on the phone, at times even addressing the operator. The voice that my students use during this activity is the best part. They are actors in the making. After 5–7 days of reading and writing 9-1-1 summaries, students review their "phone calls" and write a more in-depth summary of their reading, using the notes from this activity to guide their support and evidence.

10. The One-Minute Summary/Review

The one-minute summary serves not only as a way for students to summarize what they have read concisely, but also provides the other students in the class with some reading recommendations. This activity can be used in a station (like the directions below) or in an ongoing way, for students to complete after reading a book. The directions can be posted on a bulletin board with the cards available, and it becomes an independent reinforcer for your students. Here are the student directions for the one-minute summary/review.

Figure 3.2 9-1-1 student sample (Note that student errors have been retained for authenticity)

9-1-1 Calls

Dear operator Artie is in detenshon because of Haley and Megan is and is realy mad because she Just really Haleys dad got back from chicago and brought presents for her and Haley's sister, Haley's dad got chloe a book and said Her and Rupert could read it then cloe burst out in tears because Rupart is moving Haley over hears her mom on the phone with her aunt and her mom said she might have to plan a wedding so Haley thinks her mom and Ramon will get married or her dad and Annie will get married

Figure 3.3 One-minute book summary/review

One-Minute Book Summary/Review

Have you ever had to spend time wondering what you were going to read next? Do you want your friends to give you ideas for good books to read? That's what this station is all about!

In this station, your task is to read over the sample one-minute book reviews in the colored pockets. Then you are to look at the books you have read this year, and write one or two one-minute book reviews to share with others. Remember, a one-minute book review should not take a person very long to read, but it should contain information that will "hook" them into wanting to read your suggestion.

Steps:

- Read the one-minute book review examples to get an idea of what you should do.
- Take a blank index card from the file-folder.
- Look over your reading log to decide which book you've read you would like to recommend to others.
- Choose a colored library pocket.
- Write your one-minute book summary/review on the blank index card.
- Write your name on your colored pocket.
- Put the index card in the pocket and turn it in!
- Your one-minute book summary/review will be posted on the bulletin board for others to refer to when they are searching for a book for independent reading!

Looking Closer at Themes

The theme of a story is the message or lesson that the author wants the reader to learn from the story. Looking closely at themes and messages is found throughout the standards, but I take my time teaching this during this particular unit of study. There are many common themes:

1. courage
2. dreams
3. kindness
4. fears
5. being yourself
6. equality
7. hope
8. differences
9. friendship
10. hard work
11. honesty
12. love
13. family
14. jealousy
15. never giving up
16. doing the right thing
17. acceptance
18. peace within.

These themes, as with author's purpose, are inferred, because unless the author actually comes into the classroom or explicitly tells the reader in a side note the theme and purpose, students must rely on their background knowledge and make an educated guess. As an introductory activity, I create five index cards with a familiar theme written on each one. Next I have groups of students work together to skim and scan a short story or text, often from *Storyworks* or *Highlight* magazines, and place the selection with the correct card. By the end, my students have categorized the reading materials based on the theme. I always put a self-checking sticky note in the back of the text. I also keep baskets of books labeled by theme in my class library, and as students read a new book I may have purchased or found, they can add those books to the correct theme baskets for a year-long activity. In addition, the teacher has a little help with categorizing and organizing the reading material. Morals, lessons, and messages tie directly within the theme of a story. I have included a list of mentor texts that vary in genre as well as theme.

Using Themes to Tie in Writing Instruction

Whenever I can, which is most of the time, I incorporate writing into my reading instruction. I am, however, a firm believer that writing in a content area such as reading is critical to comprehension, but having a separate writing workshop is critical for improving writing proficiency. In order to meet the requirements of both types of writing (content area and workshop) the following writing-prompted lessons can provide students with the freedom of reflecting on their lives and backgrounds, as the workshop approach stresses, while at the same time tying in the reading standard of recognizing themes in literature.

Lesson Plan Example 1

THEME: A TIME(S) YOU WERE AFRAID
Mentor text: *Thunder Cake* by Patricia Polacco **Strategy**: Webbing
Guided practice: While listening to the mentor text, students will recall moments from their lives when the emotion of fear was present. The mentor text, *Thunder Cake*, is used for making the connection between the main character and her fear of thunderstorms.
Independent practice: Students will use a web to brainstorm moments in their lives when they were afraid. Each of these "moments" has the potential for a personal narrative seed idea.
Evaluation: Students will share with a partner a few of the moments on their web.
Conferences: Students I met with today are . . .

Lesson Plan Example 2

THEME: A TIME(S) YOU INTERACTED WITH NATURE
Mentor text: *Salt Hands* by Jane Aragon **Strategy**: Listing
Guided practice: While listening to the mentor text, students will recall moments from their lives when they had a special interaction with nature.
Independent practice: Students will create a list of moments when they interacted with nature. Beside each moment encourage students to also include feelings and visual details of the moment.
Evaluation: Students will share with a partner a few of the times with nature on their list.
Conferences: Students I met with today are . . .

Lesson Plan Example 3

THEME: A TIME(S) YOU RECEIVED A SPECIAL GIFT
Mentor text: *The Rag Coat* by Lauren A. Mills **Strategy**: Timeline
Guided practice: While listening to the mentor text, students will jot down several special gifts they have received. These gifts may or may not be linked to a holiday.
Independent practice: Students will select one moment and create a timeline of that event, concentrating on the sequence of events. Students need to include important details beside each point on the timeline. This is often referred to as "chunks of time and details."
Evaluation: Students will share with a partner some of the gifts listed on the timeline.
Conferences: Students I met with today are . . .

Lesson Plan Example 4

THEME: A SPECIAL TIME(S) SPENT WITH FRIENDS
Mentor text: *Roxaboxen* by Alice McLerran **Strategy**: T-chart
Guided practice: While listening to the mentor text, students will brainstorm a list of friends that they have spent special moments with. These names will go on the left side of a T-chart.
Independent practice: Students will look closely at each name on the left side of the T-chart. Then, on the right side of the chart, special moments spent with each friend will be listed. Encourage students to think of one friend at a time.
Evaluation: Students will share with a partner their moments with friends who were listed on the T-chart.
Conferences: Students I met with today are . . .

Lesson Plan Example 5

THEME: A TIME(S) YOU ACCOMPLISHED SOMETHING
Mentor text: *Butterfly House* by Eve Bunting **Strategy**: Quick sketch
Guided practice: While listening to the mentor text, students will brainstorm things that they have accomplished. For example, starting a food drive for shelter animals. If they had a parent or friend help them build this item, then that name needs to be included.
Independent practice: Students will evaluate the list and decide on one or two items that they emotionally connect to the most. Then students will create a quick sketch of one or two of the things that were accomplished. The quick sketch needs to be labeled with details.
Evaluation: Students will share with a partner their sketches of things accomplished.
Conferences: Students I met with today are . . .

Additional Ways to Teach Themes

The standards state that students are to compare and contrast texts based on the theme or message. The following lesson provides several mentor texts that will fit nicely within individual themes. To increase the understanding of that particular theme, I add a writing stem that asks students to reflect on their own lives based on the theme. See Table 3.1. One suggestion for adding the writing stem is to first read a mentor text a day for 3–5 days. Then add the writing stem so that students can make the personal connection.

Table 3.1 Writing Stems

THEME/WRITING STEM	BOOK TITLES/AUTHORS
Think of a special holiday(s) you remember	• *Turkey Pox* by Laurie Halse Anderson • *The Jolly Christmas Postman* by Janet and Allen Ahlberg • *The Night Before Christmas* by Natasha Wing • *The Night Before Halloween* by Natasha Wing • *Llama Llama Holiday Drama* by Anna Dewdney • *Christmas Tapestry* by Patricia Polacco • *Lady in the Box* by Ann McGovern
Think of a special time(s) spent with a relative	• *The Piano Man* by Debbie Chocolate and Eric Velasquez • *The Relatives Came* by Cynthia Rylant • *Aunt Flossie's Hats* by Elizabeth Fitzgerald Howard • *Aunt Claire's Yellow Beehive* by Deborah Blumenthal
Think of a time(s) when you traveled to a special place	• *Goin' Someplace Special* by Patricia McKissack • *Round Trip* by Ann Jonas • *The Magic School Bus* series by Joanna Cole
Think of a time(s) when you were very proud	• *Oliver Button is a Sissy* by Tomie DePaola • *I'm Proud to be Me!* by Gabriel Fitzmaurice • *The Dot* by Peter H. Reynolds

Table 3.1 *continued*

THEME/WRITING STEM	BOOK TITLES/AUTHORS
	• *Being Bella* by Cheryl Zuzo • *Shades of Black* by Sandra L. Pinkney • *Stand Tall Molly Lou Mellon* by Patty Lovell
Remember a time(s) when you helped someone	• *Duck in the Truck* by Jez Alborough • *Chips: A Hometown Hero* by Nancy M. West • *An Angel for Solomon Singer* by Cynthia Rylant • *I Can Hear the Sun* by Patricia Polacco
Remember an accident(s) or a time you got hurt	• *My Rotten Redheaded Older Brother* by Patricia Polacco • *Sam, Bangs, and Moonshine* by Evaline Ness
Remember a special shopping trip(s)	• *Anno's Flea Market* by Mitsumasa Anno • *Flower Garden* by Eve Bunting • *A Chair for My Mother* by Vera B. Williams
Think of a special time(s) you spent with a friend	• *The Tin Heart* by Karen Ackerman • *We Are Best Friends* by Aliki • *Alejandro's Gift* by Richard E. Albert • *Emma Kate* by Patricia Polacco • *The Grouchy Ladybug* by Eric Carle
Think of your worst/best day(s) at school	• *David Goes to School* by David Shannon • *Billy and the Bad Teacher* by Andrew Clements • *Bats at the Library* by Brian Lies • *Marianthe's Story: Painted Words* by Aliki
Think of a time(s) when you learned how to do something new	• *Papa's Mark* by Gwendolyn Battle-Lavert • *The Bat Boy and his Violin* by Gavin Curtis
Remember a special birthday(s)	• *Jenny's Birthday Book* by Esther Averill • *A Birthday Basket for Tia* by Pat Mora • *Birthday Monsters* by Sandra Boynton

Table 3.1 *continued*

THEME/WRITING STEM	BOOK TITLES/AUTHORS
	• *Happy Birthday to You!* by Dr. Seuss • *Some Birthday!* by Patricia Polacco
Think of a day(s) when you were very happy/sad/frightened	• *Thunder Cake* by Patricia Polacco • *Shortcut* by Donald Crews • *On the Day His Daddy Left* by Eric J. Adams • *The Wall* by Eve Bunting

Using Quotes to Tie in Themes and Messages

Thought-provoking quotes are a wonderful type of mentor text to engage students in recognizing an author's theme or message. I am a quote collector. I have five 3-inch binders filled to the brim with quotes on life, happiness, and, yes, writing and reading. I like to share quotes with my students and then, like the examples, we make personal connections and document these connections in our reader's notebooks (Table 3.2).

Thematic Conflict

So many skills in reading instruction weave themselves together and themes are no exception. If we look at the conflict found within the story, we can also uncover the theme that the literature is centrally based upon. The mentor text suggestions below are different titles from those in Chapter 2, when conflict was looked at for plot elements rather than theme.

Character vs. Character

1. *The Ugly Duckling* by Hans Christian Anderson
2. *Fiona's Lunch* by Teresa Bateman
3. *Silly Chicken* by Rukhsana Khan
4. *The Hundred Penny Box* by Sharon Mathis

Character vs. Nature

1. *The Great Kapok Tree* by Lynn Cherry
2. *Brave Irene* by William Steig
3. *The Wump World* by Bill Peet
4. *The Legend of the Bluebonnet* by Tomie DePaola

Character vs. Society

1. *Old Henry* by Joan Blos
2. *The Island of the Skog* by Steven Kellogg
3. *Wings* by Christopher Myers
4. *Have a Good Day Café* by Francis and Ginger Park

Character vs. Self

1. *Sam, Bangs, and Moonshine* by Evaline Ness
2. *Ira Sleeps Over* by Bernard Waber
3. *Thunder Cake* by Patricia Polacco
4. *The Dog Who Cried Wolf* by Keiko Kasza

Table 3.2 Quote/Connection Chart

QUOTE	POSSIBLE CONNECTION/THEME/WRITING STEM
"There are friends, I think, we can't imagine living without. People who are sisters to us, or brothers."—Julie Reece Deaver	Moments or special times with a friend or friends.
"Most smiles are started by another smile."—Anonymous	Times in your life when you made someone happy or they made you happy.
"I expect to pass through life but once. If, therefore, there be any kindness I can show, or any good thing I can do to any fellow being, let me do it now, as I shall not pass this way again."—William Penn	Random acts of kindness you showed to someone or that someone showed to you.
"Music was my refuge. I could crawl into the space between the notes and curl my back to loneliness."—Maya Angelou	Times you felt lonely or sad.
"A man should never be ashamed to own that he has been in the wrong, which is but saying . . . that he is wiser today than yesterday."—Jonathan Swift	Moments in your life when you made a bad decision and got in trouble.
"I just want to make a difference, however small, in the world."—Arthur Ashe	A time you made a difference in someone's life or they made a difference in yours.

Some Sample Thematic T-charts

I appreciate how each of the CCSS build upon each other, and I am probably the world's biggest T-chart fan. The following examples are a useful way for students to focus in on the intent of the standards and have a place to document the evidence from the text or texts. I have my students create the T-chart in the reader's notebooks, but they can be copied and used as graphic organizers as well. This evidence will be used to write summaries of their reading. Look at how the verbiage changes slightly with each grade level. Let me take a moment here to make clear that I use all of the T-charts for my fourth grade class. The spiral curriculum that the CCSS offer makes it easier to build upon and expand from the previous grade levels' expectations to the current and on to the approaching grade level's expectations. Also note that because I am working through a narrative unit (stories) of study the students will circle that genre choice on the T-chart. When we look at fables, that choice is circled, etc. These T-charts (pp. 89–91) are an excellent tool for taking notes while reading, and these notes can be beneficial when students are asked to write a summary of their daily or weekly or end on unit summaries.

Second Grade T-chart

MESSAGE, LESSON, OR MORAL OF THE *STORY*, *FABLE*, OR *FOLK TALE* (CIRCLE THE *GENRE*)	EVIDENCE FROM THE TEXT

Third Grade T-chart

MESSAGE, LESSON, OR MORAL OF THE *STORY*, *FABLE*, OR *FOLK TALE* (CIRCLE THE *GENRE*)	EVIDENCE FROM THE TEXT

Fourth Grade T-chart

THEME OF THE *STORY*, *DRAMA*, OR *POEM* (CIRCLE THE *GENRE*)	EVIDENCE FROM THE TEXT

Fifth Grade T-chart

THEME OF THE STORY, DRAMA, OR POEM (CIRCLE THE GENRE)	EVIDENCE FROM THE TEXT	EVIDENCE BASED ON CHARACTER OR NARRATOR RESPONSE

Excellent Resources for Implementing a Genre Study

I think it is important to note how the CCSS broaden literature beyond the basic narrative format. The induction of genre studies is a natural way for teachers and students to focus on particular writing styles. At the beginning of my Reading Literature study, I like to start with a basic narrative. The students are familiar with this genre. I typically spend about 7–10 days (give or take) focusing on each genre. Let me bring back my long-range planning calendar from Chapter 1. Next to each minor study within the Reading Literature unit, I add the genres I will focus on.

August:
    Introducing the Reader's Workshop (1–2 weeks)
    Questions, Inferences, and Purpose (1–2 weeks) (Chapter 2)
    Details, Summaries, and Themes (1–2 weeks) (Chapter 3)

September:
    Character Analysis and Story Elements (2 weeks) (Chapter 4)

    Craft and Vocabulary Development (2 weeks) (Chapter 5)

October:
    Structural Elements and Point of View (1–2 weeks) (Chapter 6)

    Comparing and Contrasting with Text Connections (1–2 weeks) (Chapter 6)

When I look once again at the year-long planning, I see that I will revisit Reading Literature in February. In the second rotation I will continue to add new genres for my students to read, write, and listen to during my read-aloud.

August–October
    Reading Literature (Tying in genres) (NARRATIVE: personal, POETRY, MYTHS, LEGENDS, and FABLES)

November–January
    Reading Informational Texts

February–March
    Reading Literature (Tying in genres) (NARRATIVE: fictional, PLAYS, READER'S THEATER, TALL TALES, MYSTERIES)

March–April
    Reading Informational Texts

Keeping on Track

Because introducing students to new genres and comparing those genres is an important factor with the CCSS, I keep a running chart of the books we have read (see Table 3.3). This chart is hanging up in my classroom and added to as needed. I create a new chart if I decide to work on an author study. The beauty of this chart is that it reviews so many skills that separate, longer instruction is not necessary. For example, I may spend a couple of days looking at the varied themes found in literature. Then every time a book is read and the theme is selected, I am reviewing. In this chart alone, the following skills are taught and reviewed:

- vocabulary
- theme
- genre
- author's purpose
- summarizing (the GIST).

Table 3.3 Gathering Information from Mentor Texts

BOOK TITLE & AUTHOR	NEW WORDS LEARNED	THEME, MORAL, MESSAGE	GENRE	AUTHOR'S PURPOSE	BRIEF SUMMARY THE "GIST"

Choice Board

R	E	A	D
Determine a possible theme of the story you have read. Provide evidence from the text to support your reasoning.	Summarize the story that you have just read with a "Somebody, Wanted, But, So, Then" format.	Read a poem with a partner. Both of you then summarize each stanza of the poem, then compare your summaries.	Write a story with the theme "Kindness is Always Best". Underline the evidence in your story that supports the theme.
Create a Problem/Solution T-chart. For each problem noted in the story you are reading, provide evidence from the text to support the solution.	Create a story elements graphic organizer and fill it in with the characters, setting, problem, and solution.	After each day's reading of the story, create a 9-1-1 call that focuses on the most important events and details. Use evidence from the text for support.	Read a poem. What is the main topic of the poem? How does the speaker feel during the poem? How do you know?

Closing Thoughts

I love teaching. I love organizing and creating a curriculum. I love reading different genres, and I enjoy digging deeper with my units of study. When teachers can narrow down their focus to a few comprehension skills at a time, and embed those skills within various genres, it becomes a win–win opportunity. The CCSS simply narrowed down the multitude of standards and these standards can easily be maneuvered to fit the needs of the students. It is our job, as teachers, to condense these standards into a manageable curriculum.

Chapter 4

Reading with Close Comprehension Through Character Analysis and Story Elements

"You never really understand a person until you consider the things from his point of view . . . until you climb in his skin and walk around in it."

Atticus Finch in To Kill a Mockingbird

Standard RL.3

I Can Statements

- I can use specific events and ideas from the text to explain what happened and why.
- I can identify characters, settings, and events in a story or drama.
- I can locate sections of a text where characters, setting, or events are described.
- I can use specific details from the text to describe characters, settings, or events.
- I can describe a character's traits, motivations, or feelings in a text.
- I can compare and contrast two or more characters, settings, or events in a story.
- I can determine the cause and effect of events in a story.

Figure 4.1 Another look at my notes

Chapter 4: Crate #3—White

RL.4.3: Describe a character setting or event in a story or drama, drawing on specific details in the text (a character's thoughts, words or actions).

- Character attributes/traits
- Character's actions
- Dialectal journals
- Story elements
- Visualizing the setting
- Understanding the relationships among the plot, setting, and character traits (writing to respond)
- Character analysis
- Cause and effect
- Beginning, middle, and end
- Sequencing

Character Analysis

Characters are the breathing, living element to stories. It is virtually impossible to write or read a story where characters are not present. And to be honest, who would want to? Character study is a critical component to reading comprehension. We ask our students to "connect" to what they are reading, and one way to do this is to fully understand the characters in the texts that they are reading. When teachers think about character analysis, the elements of personality, role, growth and change of the characters in the books we are using for instruction become focal points.

A Chance Meeting

In my workshops for teachers as well as in my classroom, I like to use the comparison of meeting someone for the first time and a character analysis. At first, you are virtual strangers with this person. But after a while, after interaction and conversations, you begin to determine if this "stranger" is someone you are going to like or not. Judgments are made about this person based on their physical appearance as well as character traits that are present or inferred. When we open up a new book, it is also like meeting new people. We are all "strangers" to the characters in the story. But in time, we (the readers) learn about the characters in the book, and decide if we like them or not. We decide their value in the story, and we determine if we can connect to the characters through our own personal experiences and commonalities.

Why a Unit of Study on Characters?

The Common Core State Standards in fictional literature call for students to identify characters' actions, thoughts, and motivations. This is no small task for our students. Teachers understand the importance of showing students how to carefully study characters, both major and minor ones, in a story. It is also important for students to understand that a character travels in pursuit of goals and some of these goals may be similar to their own or very different. It is easier to understand the motives of a character and predict what a character will do next or how he or she will react to a situation when this character has been analyzed during reading. Making these predictions or inferring what the "next steps" may be, are important for not only character analysis but in the comprehension of a story as well. Why? Because it involves deeper thinking about one's thinking (metacognition) and good readers deepen their understanding by walking in their characters' shoes.

Mentor Texts and Author Choices

It always amazes me how authors can make characters seem like real people. I envy writers like Patricia Polacco who can make me laugh and cry right beside the characters in her books. I actually miss them when the book is finished. As writer Alice Hoffman has shared, "After a while, the characters I'm writing begin to feel real to me. That's when I know I'm heading in the right direction." I want my students to feel as if the characters they are reading about are real.

On the other hand, there are always those characters that have negativity surrounding them, the antagonists, and students need to understand that these characters are just as important. It is these types of characters that seem just as real but add drama and suspense and conflict to a story. And what good is a book or story without conflict and drama? Here are just a few tried and true authors and mentor texts that never fail me when it comes to hearty characters. I organize my books with strong characters in labeled baskets: *Strong Character Picture Books* and *Strong Character Chapter Books*. When I first introduce the unit of study on character analysis, the books in the picture book basket are used to model my daily mini-lesson. I can typically read through one picture book a day. During independent reading the students select a chapter book from the chapter book basket and each day during the reading time, students "try-out" the mini-lesson using their own self-selected chapter book. It usually takes the entire unit of study time for them to finish the chapter books. A little later on in the year I also use a chapter book with a strong character to model each daily mini-lesson.

Possible Mini-Lessons for Character Analysis

As this chapter progresses, you will see explanations, strategies, or student samples for each of the following mini-lessons. Each mini-lesson can also be used when guiding students to write about their reading. For example, after I discuss how to choose a "just right" chapter book, my students write about *why* they chose a particular book for independent reading. And because I model every lesson first, I write in front of the students *why* I chose a particular picture book or chapter book to model the lesson. Another example would be found with mini-lesson 11. As students look closely at character traits and evidence to support those traits, enough information needs to be gathered and documented with a T-chart in the reader's notebook. After enough evidence is found, students can write a 3-paragraph summary of the three character traits most evident in the book. Another idea would be to have students create a character trait brochure using the information from mini-lesson 11 as well. There is no limit to the creative possibilities these mini-lessons offer for writing and summarizing. You can find some suggested authors and texts in Figures 4.2 and 4.3.

1. How characters drive the story
2. Main characters vs. minor characters
3. Not all characters are created equal
4. Categorizing the types of characters
5. Internal and external character traits
6. A quick sketch of external traits
7. Determining internal traits through dialogue
8. Comic strip conversations
9. Event/reaction T-chart

10. Problem/reaction T-chart
11. Trait/clue T-chart
12. Character word cloud
13. Character trait sweet rolls
14. Feelings vs. traits
15. Show don't tell using emotion cards
16. Positive and negative emotions
17. The F.A.S.T. chart
18. Character comparisons
19. Conflict-driven plot
20. Story stew
21. Fits like a puzzle
22. Plot gestures

Figure 4.2 Suggested authors

- Beverly Cleary
- Sharon Creech
- Roald Dahl
- Paula Danziger
- Patricia Polacco
- Katherine Paterson
- Gary Paulsen
- J. K. Rowling
- E. B. White
- Cynthia Rylant
- Eve Bunting

Figure 4.3 Picture books with well-developed characters

- *Ella Sarah Gets Dressed* by Margaret Chodos-Irvine
- *Today I Feel Silly and Other Moods that Make My Day* by Jamie Lee Curtis
- *Stella, Fairy of the Forest* by Marie-Louise Gay
- *Chrysanthemum* by Kevin Henkes
- *Amazing Grace* by Mary Hoffman
- *Tough Charley* by Kay Verla
- *Gooney Bird Greene* by Lois Lowry
- *Martha Walks the Dog* by Susan Meddaugh
- *Thunder Rose* by Jerdine Nolen
- *Coming on Home Soon* by Jacqueline Woodson
- *One Green Apple* by Eve Bunting
- *Pink and Say* by Patricia Polacco
- *Knots on a Counting Rope* by Bill Martin

1. How Characters Drive the Story

Many of us have met "best friends" within the pages of a book. To me, characters are the heart of a story and can either hold the story together or tear it apart. At the beginning of this unit of study, I create an anchor chart that simply asks, "How do characters drive the story?" (Figure 4.4). We take a few moments to brainstorm this question and reflect on what important roles characters play. The sample chart shows a few student responses.

2. Main Characters vs. Minor Characters

My next instructional goal, after looking at how characters drive the story, is for students to understand that there are main characters as well as minor ones. But problems can arise when they have difficulty distinguishing between the two. Sometimes my students are quick to write down any character that is first introduced in their reading, and immediately label that one as the main character. I ask them to read further and become more familiar with the characters and then distinguish between the major and minor ones. Why?

Figure 4.4 Sample anchor chart

How Do Characters Drive the Story?

- Their emotions and feelings help us connect to the story.
- They take us places and let us see them.
- They are always changing to keep the story moving along.
- They cause problems and then fix them.
- They react to events.
- They interact with other characters in the story.

It is more critical to the understanding of characterization if the major characters are the ones that a deeper study is focused around. The gentleman who helped find the puppy for a little boy in a story is important, but if that is the only time he is mentioned in the story, then picking that character to study deeper will not be effective. A T-chart like the example in Figure 4.5 is an excellent way for students to categorize the major and minor characters.

Figure 4.5 Characters T-chart

MAJOR CHARACTERS	MINOR CHARACTERS

Table 4.1 Types of Characters Found in Literature

FLAT CHARACTERS	ROUND CHARACTERS	STEREOTYPE CHARACTERS	STATIC CHARACTERS	DYNAMIC CHARACTERS	WALK-ONS
A flat character has one or two personality traits that do not change. A flat character can play a major or a minor role.	A round character has complex traits that develop and change throughout the story. A round character seems more real and believable as well as more complex. Major characters usually are considered to be round characters.	A stereotype character exists to maintain a widespread belief in the stereotypes that society has created. For example an absent-minded professor, an angry redhead, or a stingy businessman.	Static characters never change. The static characters are usually background characters. A boring character who never changes his views on life is a static character. Their role in the story will last longer than that of a walk-on character.	Unlike the static character, a dynamic character responds consistently to events and usually experiences a change in attitude or outlook. Many stories that teach a lesson involve a dynamic character.	A walk-on character is not ultimately important to the story, rather they are part of the background. In other words they are designed to fill a brief role in the story and then vanish completely out of sight.

* I use this quote by E.M. Forster (English novelist) to help students see the difference between a flat and round character: *"The test of a round character is whether it is capable of surprising in a convincing way. If it never surprises, it is flat."*

3. Not All Characters are Created Equal

No two people are alike and no two characters are either. There are many different types of characters that students will encounter (Table 4.1). The differences in characters make the book "go round." You will notice that the round and dynamic character traits are similar, as are the flat and static traits. They are basically synonymous. In K-2, I find that the flat/round verbiage is sufficient enough whereas in grades 3–5, the more advanced verbiage is welcomed and understood.

It make take several days to look closely at each type of character. I like to start with round characters because they are easier to recognize in the daily reading. *A Bad Case of Stripes* by David Shannon is an excellent text to model a round character. Figure 4.6 is a sample of the chart we created during this read-aloud. You can see how this is a great way to introduce writing about reading as well as proving points with text evidence.

Figure 4.6 Chart we created for round characters

Characterization with *A Bad Case of Stripes* by David Shannon

Round characters are well-developed and demonstrate change throughout the story. These characters are believable and memorable and have many traits, both good and bad.

Camilla is a round character because:

_____

_____

_____

_____

_____

_____

_____

_____

_____

_____

Table 4.2 Character Types

Book Title: _____

FLAT CHARACTERS	ROUND CHARACTERS	STEREOTYPE CHARACTERS	STATIC CHARACTERS	DYNAMIC CHARACTERS

4. Categorizing the types of characters

Eventually, after the different types of characters have been located, viewed, and discussed in the teacher's read-aloud of picture books or a chapter book, the instructional goal shifts to teaching students how to recognize and categorize the major and minor characters into the five character types mentioned earlier: flat, round, stereotype, static, and dynamic. I typically do not ask students to categorize the walk-on characters, but teachers certainly can if they feel that it would be beneficial to student understanding. My students are typically in individually selected chapter books during independent reading time, and notes of their reading are taken. The chart on page 104 is one example of a way for students to collect information about the characters. It is important that teachers model whatever they are asking the students to do either with a picture book, or later on in the year with an ongoing chapter book. In other words, I would show students how to fill in the chart below based on my daily reading. Remember, this task of categorizing characters may take the entire 2–3 weeks of the study because each day that students read, new information is provided to them. A simple column chart like the one in Table 4.2 can help students keep track of the character role in each day's reading.

5. Internal and External Traits

I often tell my students that we can't judge a book (or character) by the cover, but rather from the pages inside. The same is true about external character traits. I remember when I was working my way through college at a jewelry store kiosk in the local mall. The manager of the store, on my very first day on the job, reminded me that someone who walks up to the counter and looks like they are barely making ends meet could possibly turn out to be a very successful and generous loyal customer. On the same token, someone who walks up to look at jewelry dressed elaborately and dripping with jewels may not necessarily be one of our best buying customers. This conversation struck me as interesting but I didn't think about it much until several months later during the Christmas season when a gentleman with a scraggly beard, worn-out clothes, work boots that had seen better days, and a big smile on his face walked up to the counter. About the same time, a beautiful woman in a fur coat oozing designer everything walked up as well. They were both standing at my side of the jewelry counter. I liked the smile on the gentleman's face and went to his direction, whereas my co-worker chose to go to the woman in the fur coat. Long story short, I enjoyed showing the man jewelry and striking up a conversation. He was pleasant, and during this hectic holiday time that was a blessing in itself. He ended up leaving and didn't buy anything while the other customer of my coworker bought an inexpensive piece of jewelry and a small commission was earned. On an ironic note, my customer returned and bought a huge selection of jewelry

Table 4.3 Internal and External Traits

INTERNAL TRAITS (OFTEN INFERRED)		EXTERNAL TRAITS (OFTEN IMPLIED)	
active	independent	athletic	slim
afraid	intelligent	beautiful	stout
bossy	joyful	birthmarks	tall
babyish	lazy	body structure	well-dressed
bored	loving	brunette	young
bashful	loyal	colorful	
busy	mischievous	curly hair	
calm	optimistic	cute	
careful	outspoken	dashing	
cheerful	patient	expressive	
conceited	persistent	freckled	
eager	polite	hair texture	
daring	reckless	hefty	
demanding	selfish	height	
dishonest	sneaky	high-energy	
friendly	stubborn	large-boned	
gentle	suspicious	monotone	
generous	smart	petite	
greedy	timid	pretty	
hard-working	unselfish	redhead	
heroic	witty	scruffy	
impatient		short	

* Internal traits include words that describe who a person is inside, their fears, motivations, frustrations and feelings.

* External traits include a person's appearance, physical features, where they live, jobs, likes and interests. They even include mannerisms and postures, and energy level.

from me that made me the top dollar seller for the entire month, and the commission I earned bought all of my Christmas presents that year. I share this story with my students, not only for a simple life lesson, but to help them see that sometimes, even in books, assumptions are made based on initial external character traits, and that this is OK, as long as adjustments are made after further reading and the internal traits that truly make a character relevant to the story are recognized. I use the chart in Table 4.3 to help guide students with seeing the difference between the two traits.

One of my favorite mentor texts that easily compares internal and external traits is *Boundless Grace* by Vera Williams. After I have read the book, the class helps to create an anchor chart depicting Grace's traits (Figure 4.7).

Figure 4.7 Anchor chart depicting Grace's traits

Analyzing Character Traits Using *Boundless Grace* by Vera Williams

External traits

- African-American
- wears pig-tails
- has black hair
- has brown eyes
- is young
- wears American-style clothes

Internal traits

- is shy around people not in her family
- is family-oriented
- positive despite parents' divorce
- accepting of others
- eager to meet new people
- likes to travel

6. A Quick Sketch of External Traits

Since external traits are typically implied, or found within the text, a quick sketch of a character always helps solidify the difference between internal and external. I like to use a snippet from Roald Dahl's *Matilda*. The descriptions are vibrant and very detailed. You will find that this is a favorite among students. Here is a glimpse into this lesson.

Me: *Boys and girls, I know that we have been studying internal and external traits. We realize that the heart of a character is found within the internal traits, but authors definitely want readers to "see" the external difference among the characters as well. One of my favorite books,* Matilda, *by Roald Dahl, provides a descriptive physical example of a character named Ms.Trunchbull. I want us to look closely at the external details that the following passage offers. Then I want for you to draw "The Trunchbull" based solely on the words in the text.*

At that point I provide each student with an excerpt of the text that describes Ms. Trunchbull. We read the passage aloud and then I ask that all of the descriptive external traits are underlined. After that, the quick sketches begin. You can feel the excitement in the room. Students love to draw. I have found

Figure 4.8 Excerpt from *Matilda*

The Trunchbull

She was above all a most formidable female. She had once been a famous athlete, and even now the muscles were still clearly in evidence. You could see them in the bull-neck, in the big shoulders, in the thick arms, in the sinewy wrists and in the powerful legs. Looking at her, you got the feeling that this was someone who could bend iron bars and tear telephone directories in half. Her face, I'm afraid, was neither a thing of beauty nor a joy forever. She had an obstinate chin, a cruel mouth and small arrogant eyes. And as for her clothes . . . they were, to say the least, extremely odd. She always had on a brown cotton smock which was pinched in around the waist with a wide leather belt. The belt was fastened in front with an enormous silver buckle. The massive thighs which emerged from out of the smock were encased in a pair of extraordinary breeches, bottle-green in colour and made of coarse twill. These breeches reached to just below the knees and from there on down she sported green stockings with turn-up tops, which displayed her calf muscles to perfection. On her feet she wore flat-heeled brown brogues with leather flaps.

that drawing and sketching add another level to the reading and writing instruction. The boys in my classroom really become connected to a story or their own writing, when drawing is allowed. Figure 4.8 shows the excerpt from *Matilda*.

Figure 4.9 shows a sample of the words in the word study of "The Trunchbull". Figure 4.10 is a quick sketch of what students think Ms. Trunchbull looks like. After everyone has shared their quick sketch, I show a picture from the book of the actual Ms. Trunchbull and the students howl with laughter at either how close or how far they were from the real character description. This is also an excellent piggy-back writing lesson because the use of adjectives and details drives the description, and all teachers want adjectives and details in their students' writing. The higher level vocabulary in the excerpt also serves as the focal point for a word study. This study involves students looking up specific words in a dictionary to find a formal definition, locating the guide words, and recognizing the part of speech. I also ask that each new word is used in a sentence so that I can ensure that the definition is understood.

Figure 4.9 Word study from description of Ms. Trunchbull

enormous	twill	arrogant
massive	brogues	sinewy
extraordinary	smock	powerful
breeches	obstinate	cruel

7. Determining Internal Traits through Dialogue

Character traits can be inferred by looking closely at what is said. I know when I was going through school my teachers would say the "talk is cheap but actions are golden." While this may be true to some degree, when it comes to analyzing the characters in our books, dialogue carries as much weight as the actions do. Authors spend a lot of time trying to make characters come to life and seem believable. And a natural plan of action is through the dialogue. One way to help students hover over the dialogue a bit is with the use of dialectical journals (Table 4.4). In my classroom our reader's notebooks serve as the main tool for taking notes, trying out the mini-lessons and reflecting on each day's reading. I model for students how to fold a blank page in their notebooks like "a hotdog bun." Teachers who have been in

Figure 4.10 Student quick sketch of Ms. Trunchbull

110 • Character Analysis and Story Elements

Figure 4.11   Book excerpt pasted into notebook

The Trunchbull

She was above all a most formidable female. She had once been a famous athlete, and even now the muscles were still clearly in evidence. You could see them in the bull-neck, in the big shoulders, in the thick arms, in the sinewy wrists and in the powerful legs. Looking at her, you got the feeling that this was someone who could bend iron bars and tear telephone directories in half. Her face, I'm afraid, was neither a thing of beauty nor a joy for ever. She had an obstinate chin, a cruel mouth and small arrogant eyes. And as for her clothes... they were, to say the least, extremely odd. She always had on a brown cotton smock which was pinched in around the waist with a wide leather belt. The belt was fastened in front with an enormous silver buckle. The massive thighs which emerged from out of the smock were encased in a pair of extraordinary breeches, bottle-green in colour and made of coarse twill. These breeches reached to just below the knees and from there on down she sported green stockings with turn-up tops, which displayed her calf muscles to perfection. On her feet she wore flat-heeled brown brogues with leather flaps. She looked, in short, more like a rather eccentric and bloodthirsty follower of the stag-hounds than the headmistress of a nice school for children.

Table 4.4

Book title/Author: _____	
QUOTATION	**REACTION/RESPONSE/CHARACTER**
Page:	
Page:	
Page:	
Page:	
Page:	
Page:	

Written response: Look at the quotations, responses and reactions to the important quotes. Using three examples from the chart, elaborate on which character you quoted, why this quote was significant, and any predictions or reactions you had about the quote. Each example needs to be written as a separate paragraph and text evidence is required.
Example 1:
Example 2:
Example 3:

classrooms long enough know that this is a vertical fold. When we ask for students to fold a piece of paper like a "hamburger bun" it is a horizontal fold.

After the students have created a center crease on the paper, they have actually created two columns. At the top of the page above one column they write *Quotation*. At the top of the other column *Reaction/Response/Character* is written. Now during several days of reading, whenever a character in the book they are reading says something important, it is written down under the quotation column. I ask students to react to the quote in the form of a prediction, a thought as well as why the quote was significant and what was learned about that character. Again this is an excellent tool for collecting information that can be used for writing. In the chart on page 112, I added the component of writing to the bottom of the column chart.

8. Comic Strip Conversations

Students love comic strips. They are an excellent way to teach students about collecting character dialogue as well as making an inference. When the class is studying how dialogue helps to teach readers more about the characters in a book, collecting moments of dialogue is the first step. Several of the mini-lessons above have provided ways to collect this dialogue. After I have referred to the anchor charts from a previously read text, *Dog Breath* by Dav Pilkey for example, I model how a certain dialectical scene from a book can also be written in a comic strip form. At first I ask that the comic strip is illustrated in 2–3 scenes. Later on I can ask for multiple scenes and more evidence of dialogue once the students have shown they have grasped the concept. See Table 4.5.

Another way that I use comic strips is for making inferences. I photocopy a comic from the Sunday paper, and "white-out" the words. Students work with a partner and infer what words the characters in the comic strip were saying based on the facial expressions and setting. Then I show them the original comic and we see how close their inferences were.

9. Event/Reaction T-chart

Major and minor events happen throughout a story. This is what keeps the rising and falling action evident. Understanding that these logical events serve a purpose and that characters in the stories will react to these events in similar or different ways is an important concept in character analysis. I like to use the book *Dog Breath* to illustrate this point. When I am reading the

Table 4.5 Comic Strip Scene

Directions: Create a comic strip using a dialectical scene from the book you are reading. Include the dialogue that is spoken between the characters inside speech bubbles. After the comic strip scene is completed, write about why this dialogue between the characters was important to the plot of the story.
Book title/Author _____
Written response:

114 • Character Analysis and Story Elements

book aloud, I stop at certain intervals and the class helps to fill in an anchor chart. Afterwards, during independent writing, students use a blank version on the chart to document the events and reactions in the chapter book (or picture books for younger grades) they are reading. I like for the students to put a heart symbol next to the mighty major events and a star next to the minor events so that I can see that they know the difference (see Table 4.6). I use the same coding system when students are locating major and minor problems in the story. For mini-lesson 11, I included a student sample.

Table 4.6 Documenting Events and Reactions

♥ ★	EVENT	REACTION FROM THE CHARACTERS

♥ Mighty major event
★ Minor event

10. Problem/Reaction T-chart

This is the same lesson format as the event and reaction lesson above. As a matter of fact, I like to revisit the same mentor text, *Dog Breath*, but look a little closer at the major events and determine if they were indeed a problem that the characters had to face and find a solution to.

11. Trait/Clue T-chart

Any opportunity that I can find to show my students how to think through and write about their reading only helps to solidify the important roles that characters play in the pages of the books we read. After internal and external traits are looked at closely for identification, locating the evidence from the text that helped define that characters internal traits is taught. I am the world's biggest fan of the T-chart and I use this method once again to model note-taking while reading. I have included two student samples, one using the T-chart (Table 4.7) but the other using my second-favorite strategy, the four-square method (Figures 4.12 and 4.13). The same information was collected and later used in a writing assignment, I just varied the method a bit.

Table 4.7 Traits and Evidence

CHARACTER TRAIT	TEXT EVIDENCE

Figure 4.12 Student sample of the four-square method (1)

The Last of the Really Great Whangdoodles

Adjectives

① Creative
The characters and setting are made up and unusual. It sets a setting that has a singing river and its ... that ... stuff like that and its very creative.

page number 68-69

② Imaginative
There are made up worlds and 3 kids plus a professor who go to Whangdoodle land. There are interesting creatures. There's even a ... who ... colors.

page 44-45

③ Hilarious
The professor ... and ... his ... because ... don't ... there ... ... on almost hitting streetlamps and ...

page number 58-69

④ Scary
A character named the Prock ... black ... and ... scary creatures to scare ... ... also professor. Also The Prock has poison ...

page number 96-97

Character Analysis and Story Elements • 117

Figure 4.13 Student sample of the four-square method (2)

11-30-12	11 birthdays

Shocked	**Hopeful**
162-163 Amanda and Leo were shocked when her perents found them skipping school, at the mall, when they should have been at school and home sick.	160 Amanda was hopeful when she did all bad things all day that she wouln't be caught by her parents. And that she wouln't get in trouble or grounded.
Relived	**Worried**
166 Amanda was relived that her whole day repeated again after cutting class and being bad (steling scotters, going to the mall ect.) because the last night she was in big trouble for doing that stuff.	162-164 Amanda and Leo's parents were worried whe the couldn't find them and thought someone stole them because they weren't at home sick. (where Amanda should've been) Or at school (where Leo should've been.
40	

118 • Character Analysis and Story Elements

12. Character Word Cloud

I want students to become collectors of words. And when they are learning about character analysis, this collection is a direct link to character understanding. At the beginning of this study I show students various ways to read and document about the characters in the books they are reading. Many times a writing or project-based assignment follows several days of practicing a mini-lesson and taking notes in the reader's notebooks. There are times when short and sweet is the key ingredient to success. The word cloud is an example of this.

For this mini-lesson students look back over their days of reading and documenting. I ask for them to start a list of words that can describe their main character. This word list may include traits, feelings, likes, dislikes, etc. Once the list is completed, we take a trip to the computer lab. One program that the students love is wordle.com. It is a simple way for each student to create a word cloud about their character. The list each student compiles is typed into a text box, a create button is clicked and then, in a couple of seconds, a word cloud appears based on their character. We hang these up on a bulletin board display. Another twist on the wordle.com is to ask students to write a list of words describing themselves and create a cloud with that information. Students can then compare and contrast the book character and themselves for similarities and differences.

13. Character Trait Sweet Rolls

Sometimes you just have to be "sweet" to students in order to get them motivated to read and write. This easy but effective activity is a flavorful formative assessment. After students have read for several days in their chapter books, or whatever text teachers require during independent reading, and notes have been taken about the characters, the fun begins. Students look through their notes and select one character and one trait as well as the text evidence to support their inference. Using a spiral format, students create a sweet roll that represents a main character. And of course, we like to eat sweet rolls for inspiration. Figure 4.14 is a student example of a sweet roll.

Figure 4.14 Student sample of a sweet roll

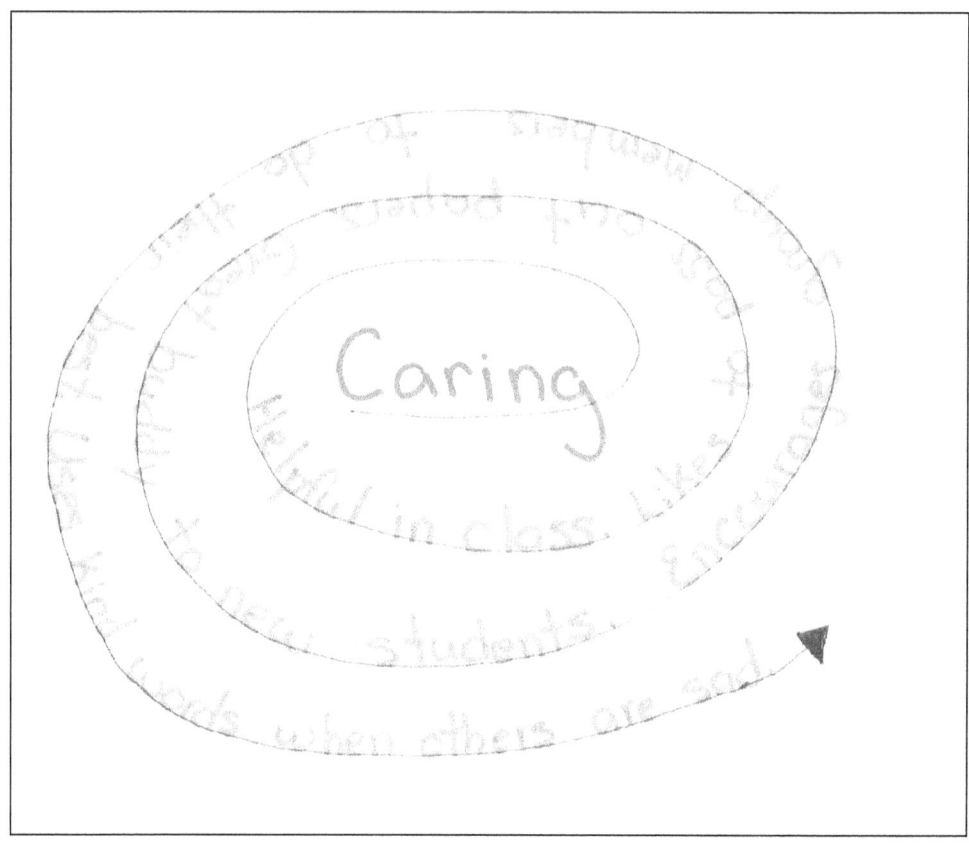

120 • Character Analysis and Story Elements

14. Feelings vs. Traits

After I have taught the differences between internal and external traits, it is time for students to look closer at the *feelings* the characters in the texts are experiencing. There is a subtle difference between feelings and traits. Character traits can be defined as someone's personality. They are words used to describe how characters act during certain situations. Character feelings are referred to as the emotional side of one's character. Even though the difference is subtle, it is important for students to identify between the two. See Table 4.8.

Table 4.8 Character Feelings and Character Traits

CHARACTER FEELINGS/ EMOTIONS		CHARACTER TRAITS	
Feelings are a character's emotional response to the actions around them.		*Traits tell us who a character is on the inside. Traits are usually seen through the actions of the character.*	
shocked	disappointed	confident	generous
exhausted	hopeful	optimistic	independent
jealous	thrilled	caring	inconsiderate
surprised	proud	kind	determined
scared	safe	nosy	mean
worried	uneasy	shy	protective
anxious	relieved	proud	patient
nervous	confused	smart	careful
excited	desperate	leader	sensitive
sad	embarrassed	brave	creative
discouraged	jealous	thoughtful	responsible
annoyed	regretful	loyal	cheerful

15. Show Don't Tell Using Emotion Cards

Emotions are the heart of the characters that students read about. A fun activity that helps students show how a character is feeling rather than just telling, takes about 5 minutes to make and will definitely create a sense of learning in the classroom. I write an emotion on an index card. I make sure that I have enough emotion cards so that each student has a chance to participate (see Table 4.9). I typically have twenty-two students. I place each index card in an empty tissue box (since we are looking at emotions!). Students break into two teams of eleven (in my room). One student from a team draws a card from the box, reads it, and uses their body and facial expressions to convey the emotion. Students from the other team that are sitting around the actor either use individual white boards or document in their reader's notebooks, the movements and expressions that were noticed. Then the "actor" calls on someone from the other team to try and guess the emotion. If a synonym of the emotion is provided as an answer, then half a point is given, if it is the correct answer, a full point is given. If, after two tries, no one in the other team makes a correct guess, the card goes back into the box. After all students have had a go, the team with the most points wins! To make it easier, I have created two sets of cards. For one set I use white index cards and all positive emotions are written on those. Then I use green index cards for the negative emotions. This helps narrow down the options for the players. Also it helps to tape the correctly answered cards to the whiteboard so that the answer is not repeated.

Table 4.9 Sample Emotion Card

Angry	Eyes narrowed Feet stomped Arms folded in front of chest

16. Positive and Negative Emotions

Piggybacking on mini-lesson 15, I have students categorize the emotions into positive and negative T-charts. Afterwards, two groups are formed, one a positive group and the other a negative group. Then one group member lies down on a large piece of butcher paper and his body outline is traced. A "face" is created that displays which type of emotions the group is working on. For the positive emotion group, a wide smile and happy features are drawn, if it is the negative emotion group, then unhappy features are added to the face. It is then time for the groups to write the appropriate emotions that have been collected, as well as those thought about during this activity, all around the body outline. These two student-created charts are hung on the walls as anchor charts that are added to and referred to throughout the year.

17. The F.A.S.T. Chart

Once characters' feelings, actions, sayings and thoughts have separately been taught and modeled, "putting the pieces together" in a four-square strategy gives students multiple tasks to think about during their independent reading time. I tell students to "think fast" while they are reading!

For the F.A.S.T. chart, I typically allow 5–7 days for reading and documenting before I assign a written response. The written response might be a 5-panel brochure or a 5-paragraph essay using the format in Figure 4.15.

Figure 4.15 5-paragraph format

Paragraph/Panel 1:	Introduction
Paragraph/Panel 2:	Focus on the feelings using text evidence
Paragraph/Panel 3:	Focus on the actions using text evidence
Paragraph/Panel 4:	Focus on the sayings using text evidence
Paragraph/Panel 5:	Focus on the thoughts using text evidence

Here is the breakdown of the F.A.S.T. acronym:

F—Feelings
A—Actions
S—Sayings
T—Thoughts.

Figure 4.16 F.A.S.T. chart

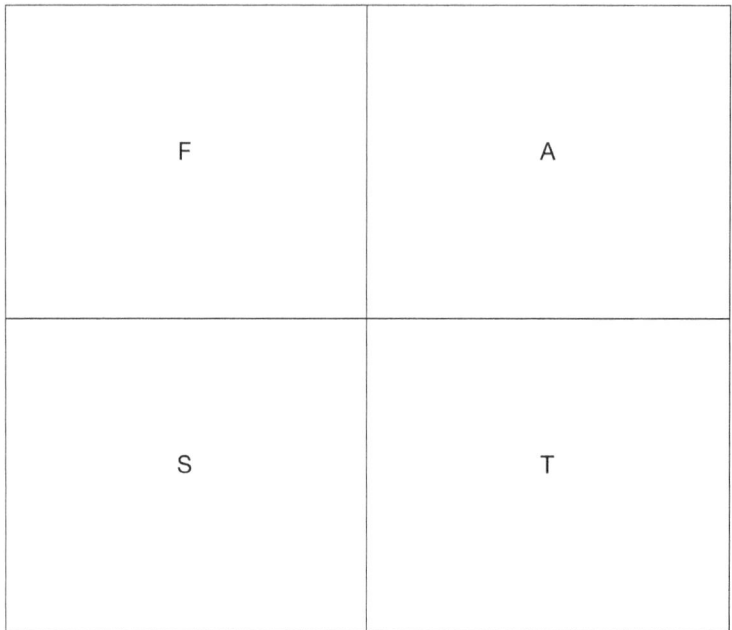

Having students create a simple four-square chart in their reader's notebooks for each day during independent reading is a quick and efficient way of evidence-collecting (see Figure 4.16). I always stress the importance of adding page numbers to any evidence in their notes. This becomes helpful when a writing assignment is linked to the notes and evidence. It can be a painstaking process watching students try and find where a major scene or quote was, without that page number.

By this point of the year, I have switched to using chapter books to model most of the character analogy mini-lessons. There is no definitive time to switch from picture books to chapter books for the read-aloud. This is completely at the teacher's discretion and is based on age, grade level, and readiness.

One of the best chapter books I have found for this F.A.S.T. lesson is *A Taste of Blackberries* by Doris Buchanan Smith. The rich text, strong characters, and emotional connection that the book offers also makes it an excellent resource for the emotional roller coaster as well as character comparisons and traits. As a matter of fact, I can't think of a single mini-lesson that this book could not demonstrate.

18. Character Comparisons

Once again, a simple column comes to the rescue. Comparing characters and looking for similarity as well as differences is an important layer of understanding within the unit of study. To begin this mini-lesson, I model the process using two student volunteers from my class. A large 3-column chart is created on the whiteboard. I am not a big fan of the Venn diagram because, in my observations, it seems more difficult for all of the information to be recorded. That middle section for *similarities* is just never quite large enough, so we like to use a 3-column chart like the one below, but whatever format is chosen is fine, it is the understanding of the lesson that is important.

After two students have been selected, and the sample chart has been filled in with information on the similarities and differences, it is time for the students to create their own 3-column chart in their reader's notebooks. The goal is to collect information while reading and fill in the columns based on two characters and the text evidence found to support the information. This is an ongoing lesson because every day that the students read, more information and evidence to back that information is located. It is easy to see how a 'compare and contrast' essay could be written after enough information has been collected.

The column chart sample looks like the example in Table 4.10.

Table 4.10 Character Comparison Chart

CHARACTER NAME:		CHARACTER NAME:
Differences	Similarities	Differences

19. Conflict-driven Plots

Everyday life has conflict. The stories students read have conflict as well, and this conflict is what can drive the plot. A *plot-driven story* is one in which a character takes a particular action so that the result is a particular plot point. Earlier we looked at how characters drive a story. A *character-driven plot* is when something about the character's "self" leads to a particular action or event in the story. For grade 2–3 classes, this information may not be necessary information, but for grades 4 and 5, the comparison of these two types of plots would be more relevant. In Chapter 3 I described how this conflict can also be considered part of the theme or message. Here, I want to only look at how it controls the plot. Many of the titles below are different from the list provided in Chapter 3. Let's look a little closer at four different types of conflict that can be found in texts.

Character vs. Character

The Ugly Duckling by Hans Christian Andersen
Fiona's Lunch by Teresa Bateman
Rumpelstiltskin by Brothers Grimm
Snow White and the Seven Dwarves by Brothers Grimm
A Bargain for Frances by Russell Hoban
Silly Chicken by Rukhsana Khan
Harriet and the Promised Land by Jacob Lawrence
The Hundred Penny Box by Sharon Mathis
The Tale of Peter Rabbit by Beatrix Potter
The Basket Moon by Mary Lyn Ray
Angel Child, Dragon Child by Michele Maria Surat

Character vs. Nature

High as a Hawk by T. A. Barron
Coyote Cry by Byrd Baylor
The Great Kapok Tree by Lynn Cherry
The Legend of Bluebonnet by Tomie DePaola
The Lorax by Theodor Geisel (Dr. Seuss)
Ming Lo Moves the Mountain by Arnold Lobel

Stella and the Berry Thief by Jane B. Mason

The Last Dinosaur by Jim Murphy

The Wump World by Bill Peet

Peggony Po: A Whale of a Tale by Andrea Davis Pinkney

Papi's Gift by Karen Stanton

Brave Irene by William Steig

Character vs. Society

Old Henry by Joan Blos

The Island of the Skog by Steven Kellogg

Chachaji's Cup by Uma Krishnaswami

The Story of Ferdinand by Muro Leaf

Wings by Christopher Myers

The Biggest Bear by Lynd Ward

Character vs. Self

Darkness and the Butterfly by Ann Grifalconi

The Dog Who Cried Wolf by Keiko Kasza

Sam, Bangs and Moonshine by Evaline Ness

Thunder Cake by Patricia Polacco

Ira Sleeps Over by Bernard Waber

The Parrot Tico Tango by Anna Witte

Hey, Al by Arthur Yorinks

After reading several examples of each type of character conflict, modeling how to collect evidence of this conflict during reading is important. The chart in Table 4.11 is used to record this relevant information about conflict.

Table 4.11 Collecting Evidence

Name of character:	
What problems and/or challenges does this character face?	*How does the character react to these problems/challenges?*

Writing Stem:
How do the problems or challenges the character faces help you determine the type of conflict in the story? Use the text evidence from the story to support your answer.

20. Story Stew

Here is a sample of a lesson plan (Figure 4.17) that will incorporate both story elements of character and setting. Even though this lesson aligns closely to a fictional narrative, do not bypass using it for a personal narrative as well. Remember, with just a little "tweaking" of the lessons and strategies in this book, both types of narrative writing can easily be taught.

It is important for students to realize that a strong sense of character and setting will lure the reader into their world and, once there, it is the role of the writer to keep them there with details, action and climax.

21. Fits Like a Puzzle

As with the story stew strategy, making the connection between the characters and the setting is important. The chart below (Figure 4.18) shows a basic setting and the characters that are likely to be found there. Students can keep a similar chart in their reader's notebooks to document the different settings and characters they find during their independent reading. One of the many reasons that I like for students to read chapter books is because of the variations of characters and settings that they can find within one book. After the students have a feel for the characters and setting, they create puzzles based on the book they are reading. Typically their chapter books have two to three main characters and two to three main settings. Students draw enough puzzle pieces on notebook paper to represent each section. For example, if a student has three main characters and two main settings, then five puzzle pieces would be drawn. Inside each puzzle piece, a description is written and an illustration provided. The puzzles are cut apart, placed in envelopes or ziplock bags and shared with the other students. If a student has read the book before, it is a great review, but if they haven't read the book, the puzzle may be the spark that makes them write the title down in their *"Want to Read"* chart in their reader's notebook.

Figure 4.17 Sample lesson plan

STORY STEW

Materials required: apron, cooking pot, wooden spoon, storybook, index cards

Activity time: 20 minutes

Concepts taught: characters, plot, setting

To begin, the teacher dons an apron and produces the cooking pot and spoon and tells the students they are going to make story stew. Explain that a good story is like stew—it has lots of ingredients.

Reach into the pot and pull out an index card on which you have written "characters." Explain that characters are "Who is the story about?" Mention familiar stories and ask students to tell you who the characters are.

Reach into the pot and pull out another index card on which you have written "setting". Explain to the students that the setting is "When and where the story happens." Mention familiar stories and ask the students to identify the setting.

Reach into the pot and produce a final index card on which you have written "plot". Explain that plot is "What happens in the story." Mention familiar stories and ask the students to briefly explain the plot.

After this introduction, read a story of your choice to the students. (I like to use *Officer Buckle and Gloria* by Peggy Rathmann, but any story with few characters, a well-defined setting, and a simple plot will suffice.) After reading the story, ask the students to identify the characters. Write them on an index or recipe card and drop it into the cooking pot. Stir it up. Then ask students to identify the setting and the plot in the same manner. After stirring up the "ingredients", reach into the pot and produce a photocopy of the cover of the story you have just read.

Follow-up ideas: Ask students to create their own "story stew" by having them make up characters, a setting, and a brief plot description and write it on a recipe card. Then have the students develop a story using their elements. Or, for a center idea, provide recipe cards with story elements written on them and let students choose one to write a story about.

---

* Remember that the setting of a story includes the year, geographical location (city, state, and country), season, culture, time of day, and place.

Figure 4.18 Settings and characters

Settings and Characters
✶ Fit Together like a Puzzle ✶

Settings	Characters
desert	lizard, snake, Indiana Jones
Alaska	owl, husky, polar bear, eskimo
tropical island	birds, hula dancer, fire ants
school	students, principals, teachers
farm	horse, farmer, cat, milkers
shopping mall	people: cashiers ? consumers
Mars	aliens/martians, astronauts
Columbus	Brutus, our governor
Cedar Point	children, Mr. Milford, parents
Disney World	Woody, Mickey, Buzz, Chip

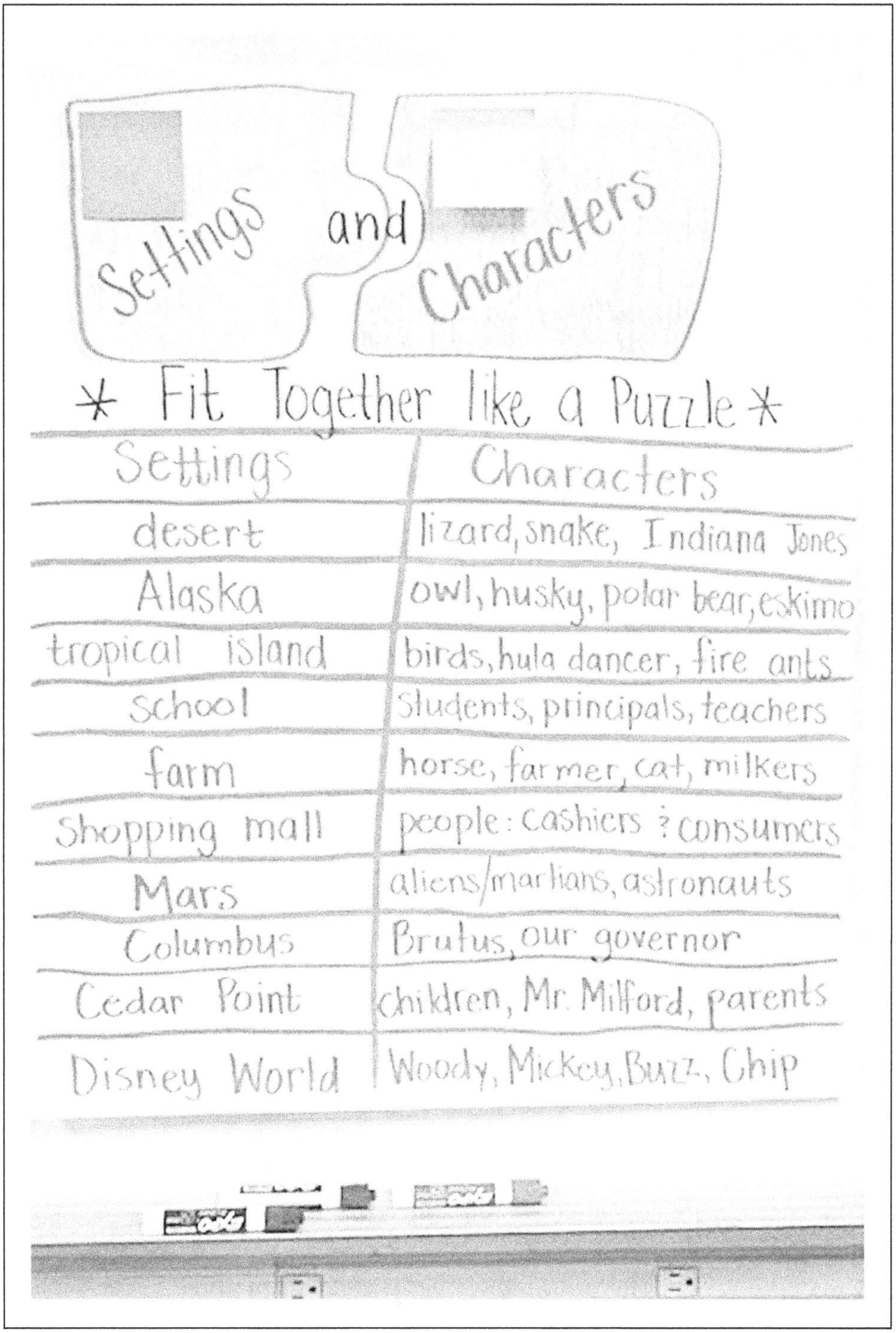

Teaching Plot and Conflict Development

The element of plot is always one of my favorite areas to teach. I enjoy the rising and climactic moments that a well-written story produces. The definition of plot is simply the main events of a story devised by the writer in a sequential order. This sequential order involves the following five steps:

1. Exposition (Brilliant Beginning)
2. Rising Action (Mighty Middle)
3. Climax (Mighty Middle)
4. Falling Action (Mighty Middle)
5. Resolution (Exceptional Ending)

The following plot gestures are an excellent way to introduce the sequential order of events found in most stories. My students like to get up and move around and I believe that when their bodies are moving, their brains are better absorbing the information.

22. Plot Gestures

Exposition—Introduces the characters, the setting, and the problem.
Have students cross their arms in an X position in front of their faces and then rest their chins on their X. Then have them turn their heads left to right and make silly faces. You want them to "act like characters." Have students repeat the words "Characters, setting, problem!" over and over again while making the gestures.

Rising action—The sequence of events that led up to the problem or conflict.
Have students squat and then gradually stand up while chanting, "Rising, rising, rising ACTION!" It always helps if they use a silly voice or accent.

Climax—The most exciting part of the story, the turning point.
Have students place their arms above their head and say "Climax!" Then have the students reach as high as they can towards the ceiling.

Falling action—Immediately follows the climax. It is where the problems begin to unwind.
While standing, students gradually lower back to a squatting position while whispering "Falling, falling, falling action."

Resolution—The problems are worked through, lessons learned, and the story is concluded.

Have students rub their hands together as if "wiping them clean" and say "Resolution." Another gesture for this would be to have the students make the motion of windshield wipers with their arms. Also as if saying "Wiping it clean."

After several practices with the plot gestures, it is time for the students to independently recognize and document events in the texts they are reading. Figure 4.19 shows a simple "roller coaster" organizer that I find helps students with this documentation. Figure 4.20 shows my sample for modeling the plot. As usual, what I teach in the reading workshop will directly help in the writer's workshop. If students understand the sequence of events and plot in something they are reading, when it comes time to write sequentially, with plot-driven narratives, their job as a writer becomes a little easier.

Figure 4.19 Graphic organizer for modeling the plot

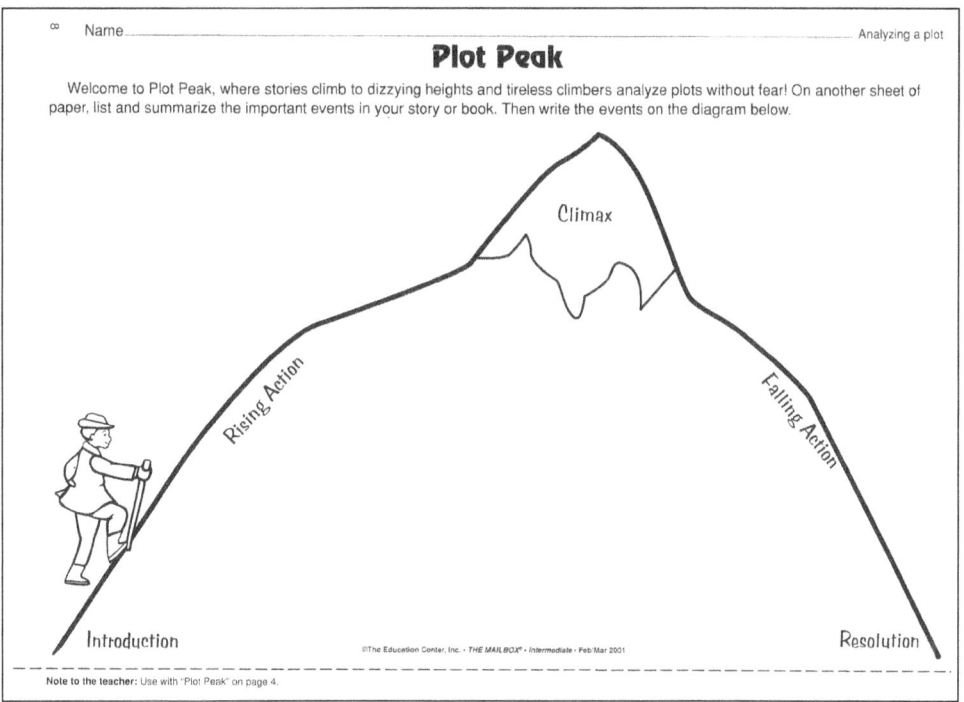

Figure 4.20 My teaching sample

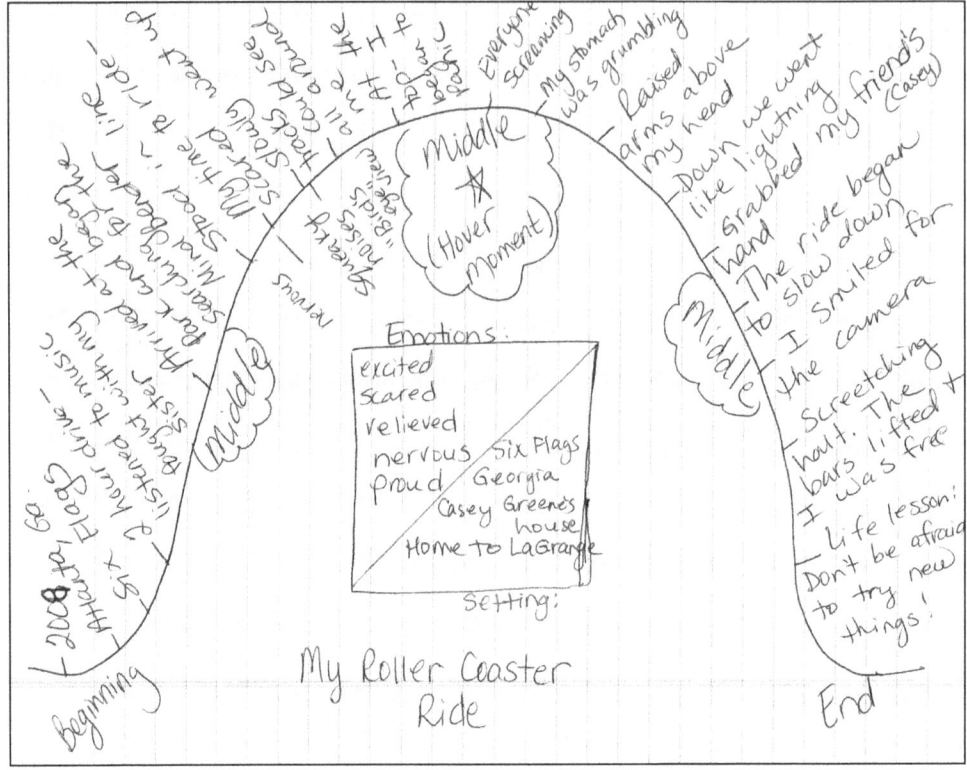

Cause and Effect

Cause and effect relationships are a basic part of the curriculum and can be taught in all subjects. For reading literature, however, I look at the three basic types of cause and effect relationships and popular mentor texts that can be used for modeling.

1. **Stated cause and effect**—This is clearly stated in the story.

    The Runaway Bunny by Margaret Wise Brown

2. **Unstated cause and effect**—Students will need to read between the lines.

    Tops and Bottoms by Janet Stevens

3. **Reciprocal cause and effect**—One effect will cause a second one and so on ... also referred to as a circular story.

    If You Give a Mouse a Cookie by Laura Numeroff

Signal Words

Teaching students to look for (but not rely on) signal words can help them understand a cause and effect relationship in the text they are reading. Figure 4.21 shows a few signal words to point out during modeling. Figure 4.22 shows suggested mentor texts.

Figure 4.21 Signal words

- because
- so
- if
- then
- as a result of
- may be due to
- therefore
- the reason why

Figure 4.22 Mentor texts for teaching cause and effect

- *Cloudy With a Chance of Meatballs* by Judi Barrett
- *A House for a Hermit Crab* by Eric Carle
- *Who Wakes Rooster?* by Clare Hodgson Meeker
- *The Giving Tree* by Shel Silverstein
- *How I Became a Pirate* by Melinda Long
- *The Stray Dog* by Marc Simont
- *Twilight Comes Twice* by Ralph Fletcher
- *Miss Nelson is Missing* by Harry Allard
- *That's Good! That's Bad!* by Margery Cuyler
- *Shortcut* by Donald Crews

Organizers for Documenting Cause and Effect Relationships

I can never have enough ways for my students to collect information in their reading. I like simple charts that the students can draw themselves (see Tables 4.12–4.14). Just about everything the students do is documented in their reader's notebooks. Many times, if a chart is more multi-step, I shrink a sample of the chart to 85 percent and it is glued into the back of the notebooks as a reference. Any organizers that I have provided in this book can be used the same way. The students do not write on the blank organizer, it is just salvaged at the back for future use and reference.

Table 4.12 Happening/What Made it Happen T-chart

HAPPENING	WHAT MADE IT HAPPEN
List four events from your reading	*Then tell what made each event happen*
1.	
2.	
3.	
4.	

Table 4.13 Cause and Effect Matrix

CAUSE OF	EVENT	EFFECT OF

* Students are reminded to keep the events in order based on the book they are reading. I suggest that each event is numbered. This helps with sequencing and plot structure. Often, as students get closer to the climax, the events, causes, and effects become more numerous. A summary can be written using this matrix as well.

Table 4.14 Causes and Consequences for an Effect

Directions: Give two causes and one consequence for each event.
EVENT 1: Happens
Because
Because
Consequence:
EVENT 2: Happens
Because
Because
Consequence:

* After several days of reading in their chapter books, students need to determine and select two major events that have happened. Then after several more days of reading, the process can be repeated. Using this chart, students can then write a summary of events.

The Domino Effect

Using the following graphic organizer (Table 4.15), students choose a "cause" and write about how it affects them, their family, their community, and the world. This is a great example of how to tie in a writer's workshop assignment with what is also being learned in the reader's workshop. You can also see how current events as well as the social studies and science curriculum can fit in nicely.

Table 4.15 Graphic Organizer for the Domino Effect

CAUSE:
How does this affect self or family?
How does this affect the community?
How does this affect the world?

* Some possible topics to consider: global warming, immigration, pet welfare, pollution, natural disasters, inventions, presidential elections, etc.

Choice Board

R	E	A	D
Create a 3-column graphic organizer to describe the characters, setting and plot of your story in depth.	Choose a main character from your story. Describe the character in depth using examples of character thoughts, words, traits, and actions.	Choose an important event from your story. Describe the event in at least five sentences using details from the story.	Create a B-M-E (beginning, middle, and end) column chart and in each column explain the key events you read from the story.
Create a cause and effect T-chart. Include at least three events and three causes of the event using key details from the story.	Create a word web with words describing the main character. Use explicit details from the text to complete the web.	Create a quick sketch of the main character. Use labels to describe specific details of the character. Use evidence from the text in your quick sketch.	Read a play. Describe the most important scene in at least five sentences. Include the reasons you think that this scene is important.

Closing Thoughts

Teaching students the value of character analysis and story elements and cause and effect ensures that they will probably never look at the pages of their books quite the same way again. Teachers understand that a unit of study on these skills will more than likely take 2 weeks, and then more than likely be revisited again in the year for an additional 2 weeks. This helps relieve the pressure that everything must be taught at once. The mini-lessons in this chapter are more than enough to complete two cycles of study, or to complete one cycle and use the other mini-lessons as review throughout the year. The important thing to remember is that a teacher who teaches prescriptively, and focuses on what the students need, will teach with depth and not just coverage.

Chapter 5

Reading Closely to Recognize the Importance of Craft and Vocabulary Development

"Reading, as I am describing it, is not a treasure hunt for the main idea; it is a journey we take with a writer."
                                                        Thomas Newkirk

Standards RL.4 and RL.7

I Can Statements

- I can make meaning of words and phrases, when reading about characters in a myth, story, poem, or song, by using clues found within the text.
- I can use various strategies to determine the meanings of words and phrases.
- I can recognize words in a text that allude (refer) to characters found in mythology, stories, poems, or songs.
- I can make connections between text types.
- I can recognize when a visual or oral presentation is based on a text.
- I can identify where a text gives specific descriptions and directions that a visual or oral presentation uses.
- I can determine similarities and differences between a written text and its visual or oral representation.

Figure 5.1 Another look at my notes

Chapter 5: Crate #4—Black

RL.4.4: Determine the meaning of words and phrases as they are used in a text, including those that allude to significant characters found in mythology (Herculean).

- Figurative language
- Descriptive language
- Document details to show character's traits
- Understanding the connotative use of words (own don't rent words)
- Genre-mythology (fourth grade)
- Feelings and sensory awareness
- Word choice
- Vocabulary enrichment
- Visualization
- Genre selections

RL.4.7: Make connections between the text of a story or drama and a visual or oral presentation of the text, identifying where each version reflects specific descriptions and directions in the text.

- Text features (for narrative)
- Visualizing
- Derive information from graphics and text (mood and tone)
- Artistic interpretations
- Connections with the text
- Illustrations
- Artist studies

The Craft of Writing

Words. Words. Words. I love them. I love to write them and read them. I appreciate the effort it takes to get them on paper. And when the words paint a picture or create a feeling inside me, I know that the writer did a good job. It is this *craft* of language that engages readers and not just for comprehension or for a state test, but for a lifetime. I want to help create lifelong readers.

I have often wondered how many students have turned away from the enjoyment of reading because of the curricular demands that are placed on the teacher and then ultimately the students. Are teachers too busy to let students read for enjoyment? Is everything so fast-paced that students fail to see the beauty of the words they are reading? At home do they pick up a book from their shelves that is not an assigned reading? I ponder these questions in my head all of the time. Of course I value reading with intent and purpose, but that intent and purpose isn't always based on a test or an assignment. Can't that purpose be for enjoyment? Are we teaching our students to not only embrace the craft of language but also recognize its importance? Or are we micro-managing them to read and stop and code with a certain symbol and lose the flow of their thoughts? In other words, isn't it OK to slow down a little and let students absorb the reading first and then show them how to reflect on their reading and finally learn to write and respond to their reading?

I know, for me, that even if a task is difficult, I will stick to it if I enjoy what I am doing and see results. Let me equate this thought process to my strength training. For 3 hours a week I lift weights. Sometimes it is fun and sometimes it is not. If the only reason I went through this regimen each week were to pass a fitness test or because my trainer told me I had to, I am not sure how long I would stick with it. Now, if I was allowed to pick out a large percentage of the exercises I would like to do (I am) and if I was given adequate time to practice these exercises (I am), and more importantly, if I was allowed to start with a "just right weight limit" and know that I would increase that limit with many opportunities for practice (I am), and finally, if I could see the results of my efforts (I can) then I may become a lifelong strength trainer (I will).

How does this fit into the craft of writing and reading literature? Because when we teach our students to recognize a writer's intentional (and sometimes unintentional) use of creative language, we are teaching them to notice the *literary devices* as well as the *figurative language* in the text. This provides intent and purpose as well as adding to the enjoyment of reading a good book. But there is a balance between analyzing the words and phrases and making the entire process feel more like a chore.

I can still remember being asked to "tear apart" the poetry of Emily Dickinson. My professor analyzed and re-analyzed every aspect of her poems. At one point, after spending many class sessions on one poem in particular, I finally asked if maybe she picked a rose as a symbol, because, well, she just liked the rose. My thoughts then were as they are now, does every word or phrase have to be dissected? And is more always better? And because most authors we read will never come into our classrooms to discuss their writing, isn't most of the meaning conveyed basically inferred, and variations of thoughts and interpretations of the language acceptable?

Reading like a Writer

"Reading like a writer" is a phrase that means to carefully examine what you read, not just for content but to study the "writerly" techniques. When I first started teaching, content and comprehension were the big push. It was a teacher's task to have students read and answer questions, again and again. It was rare that I asked my students to notice the beauty of the words they were reading or apply this craft of language in their own writing. This type of instruction where students make important connections between reading and writing was not a major factor of the curriculum.

About twelve years ago, when writing instruction became a larger piece of the "curriculum pie," I had a good bit of learning and relearning I had to do with regard to the craft of language, and as I began to show my students the figurative language and literary devices, I was basically relearning them myself. Now, not only do I read like a writer in my classroom, I am aware of the creativity I see in my own self-selected reading and personal writing. It has become second nature.

I recently read an excellent memoir, *Wild*, by Cheryl Strayed. In this poignant story, there were numerous moments of what writers call the craft of language: similes, metaphors, strong emotions, show don't tell, personification, and so forth. While I was reading this book, I didn't stop and jot down all examples of craft that I recognized, but I was aware of their presence and the impact they made on me as a reader. That awareness is reading like a writer, and that awareness shows deeper understanding of the language that is also important to comprehending the text.

As a teacher, I am constantly thinking in my head how something I see or read may play an important part in my teaching. When I do come across a section from my personal (or professional) reading that oozes, "I must share this with my students" then I bookmark it with a sticky note and bring it to class the next day. The deeper our study of the craft of language becomes, the more I find that my students will excitedly do the same thing with books they are reading in class or at home. It always brings a smile to my face when a student bursts through the door with a sticky note flapping from the top of a book. I know that this little strip of paper is marking a page that models an example of the type of craft that we are studying or have studied in class. This is when I know real learning has taken place, and awareness and connections to the language that is being read have been made. When students read like a reader, they are reading for comprehension, and when they read like a writer, they are reading in order to learn about writing. This knowledge of writing does not only apply to what is noticed in a text that is written by someone else, it applies to adding this noticing to their own writing. This is where the major shift with regard to the reading and writing curriculum comes into play—the CCSS.

Teaching Students to Notice Craft of Language

For me, noticing and modeling are always the first steps with anything that I teach. And one of the best times to notice and model is during a daily read-aloud. This noticing and modeling is not just applied during the reading workshop instruction but also during the writer's workshop instruction as well, and just as importantly, it is applied during the social studies instruction. If I taught science, you would find it there as well. In other words, any time a teacher picks up a book or a poem or any type of text example, the opportunity is there to read like a reader and then reread like a writer. With the importance and focus in most schools on close reading in the reading curriculum as well as in the content areas of science, social studies, and even math, this noticing and modeling through multiple readings of a text has become an integral part of the curriculum and I am glad that is has, but, again, there is a balance between noticing and overemphasizing. Personally, I embrace close reading as a way to focus students' attention on the craft and structure of the language found in the text examples they are reading. I enjoy finding a variety of texts that not only support the core comprehension strategies but also support the many craft of language examples that are being taught in classrooms. But I also appreciate when students are reading like writers in their self-selected books as well.

Four Categories of Craft

There are four categories of craft: **(1) word, (2) audible, (3) structural,** and **(4) visual**. These categories cover what the CCSS refer to as *craft* and *structure*. When I look at craft and structure as a reader, I am noticing what an author has modeled in their work. I think of craft (language) as a major part of the *revising step* when aligned to the writing process in the writing instruction and the structure as more aligned with the *publishing step* of the writing process. In my opinion, both elements add to the creativity of a piece of writing. In this chapter, I chose to combine two standards, RL.4 and RL.7. Standard 4 is under the domain of craft and structure while standard 7 is under the domain of integration of knowledge and ideas. I put these two standards together in a unit of study because they both deal with artistic elements. Before I elaborate on the four categories of craft, let's review the craft and structure verbiage of the standard.

Craft and Structure
CCSS.ELA—Literacy.RL.4
Interpret words and phrases as they are used in a text, including determining technical, connotative, and *figurative meanings*, and analyze how *specific word choices* shape meaning or tone.

Sometimes, for me, it is easier to categorize what needs to be taught in order to make sure all of the bases are covered. One of the best books that I have found that looks closely at all four of categories of craft with regard to both language and structure is *Cracking Open the Author's Craft* by Lester Laminack. In this resource book, Laminack takes a close look at one of his own picture books, *Saturdays and Teacakes*, and models his writing decisions. He also gives insight on how and why each use of craft was chosen. In this book, I look closely at the specifics of the creativity found in the *word* and *audible* craft categories.

1. **Word—careful and deliberate word choice**
   - sensory words/imagery
   - vivid verbs
   - figurative language (simile, idioms, hyperbole, personification)
   - parallel structure

2. **Audible craft—sound choices**
   - alliteration
   - assonance
   - onomatopoeia
   - repetition
   - dialogue

3. Structural—framework of the writing

- text structure
- paragraph types
- transitional devices
- repetition
- page layout

4. Visual craft—print features

- line breaks
- white space
- illustrations
- creative texts

Activities and Mentor Texts for Teaching Word Craft

Sensory Images

The senses are a direct way for students to connect with what they are reading. When the use of multiple senses evokes a picture in the reader's mind, we call this imagery. Starting off the year, each of the senses will need to be reviewed (or introduced in the younger grades) and hovered over for a deeper understanding of the craft language needed to bring each individual sense to life. The descriptive nature of sensory details conveys an image to the reader and we want our students to recognize when they have come across such language. Stephen King sums up this point perfectly when he says, "Description begins in the writer's imagination, but should finish in the reader's."

The following organizational chart (Table 5.1) provides students with a place to recognize the use of sensory details, and I also use the same type of chart when I am modeling the strategy with a read-aloud.

I believe in the power of a mentor text. Close by my side during an introduction or review of sensory images is a basket of the books shown in Figure 5.2.

Table 5.1 Sensory Image Scavenger Hunt

Book title:		
SENSE/PAGE #	**WORDS I FOUND**	**IMAGES IN MY MIND**
See		
Hear		
Smell		
Taste		
Touch		

Figure 5.2 Mentor texts for teaching sensory images

Night Sounds, Morning Colors by Rosemary Wells

The Popcorn Book by Tomie DePaola

The Listening Walk by Paul Showers

The Ghost-Eye Tree by Bill Martin Jr.

Knots on a Counting Rope by Bill Martin

Twilight Comes Twice by Ralph Fletcher

A Day on the Prairie by Illinois third grade students of Kildeer Countryside Elementary School in Long Grove*

Night Noises by Mem Fox

Night in the Country by Cynthia Rylant

Hello Ocean by Pam Munoz Ryan

Miss Rumphius by Barbara Cooney

Soft and Smooth, Rough and Bumpy: A Book About Touch by Dana Meachen Rau

Yum! A Book About Taste by Dana Meachen Rau

---

* Each year Scholastic has a contest for schools to write books, they select a couple, and publish them.

The beautiful thing about teaching the craft of language in the reader's workshop, is you can also piggy-back the lesson in the writer's workshop. There are so many ways to tie in the senses in a reading and writing lesson but here are a few of my reliable favorites. Student samples are shown in Figures 5.3 and 5.4.

- popping popcorn (I use the book *The Popcorn Book* for this lesson);
- taking a sensory walk around the school (I use the book *The Listening Walk* for this lesson);
- taste test of unusual foods (I use the book *Yum! A Book About Taste* for this lesson);
- mystery bags each filled with different items (rice, play dough, cooked pasta) (I use the book *Soft and Smooth, Rough and Bumpy: A Book About Touch* for this lesson).

Figure 5.3 Popcorn writing sample

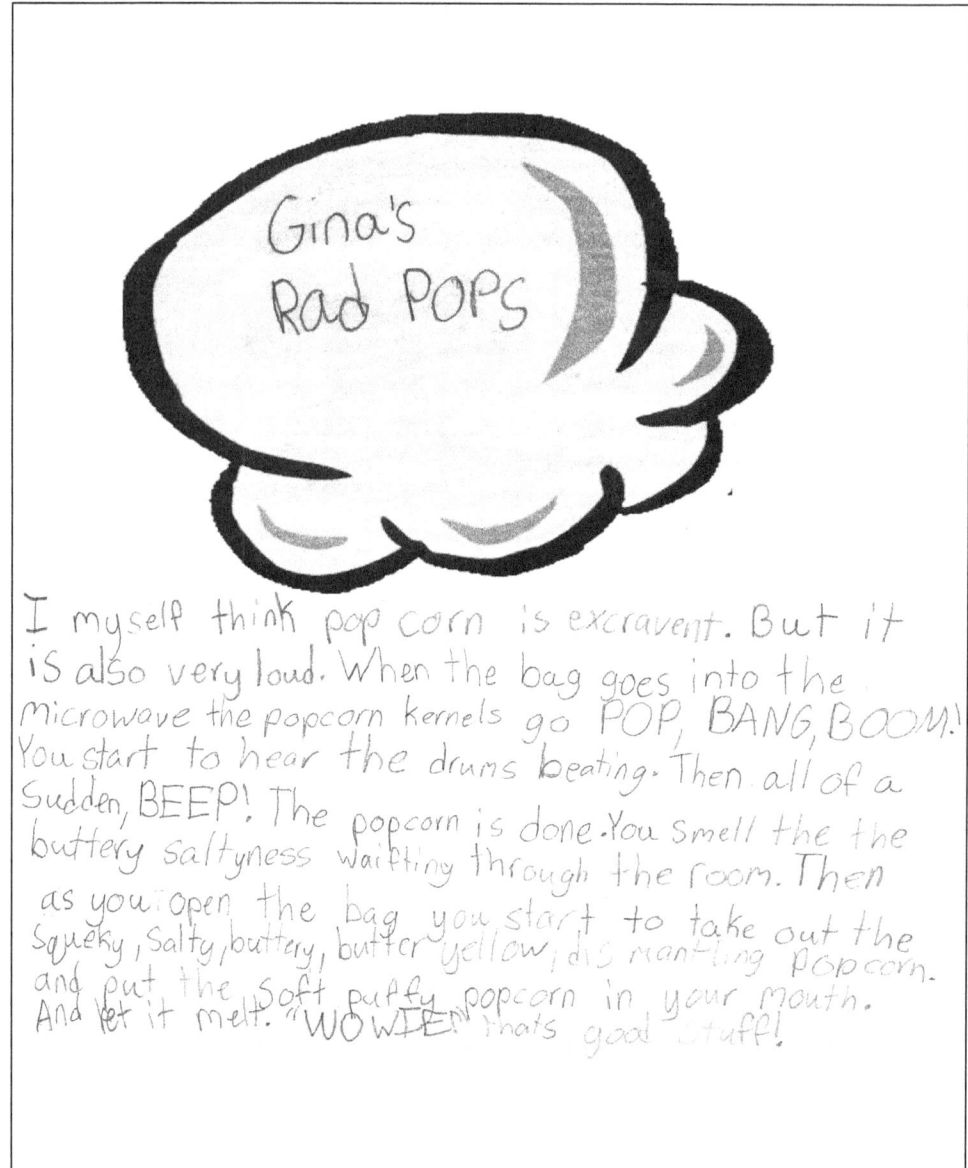

Gina's Rad POPs

I myself think pop corn is excravent. But it is also very loud. When the bag goes into the microwave the popcorn kernels go POP, BANG, BOOM! You start to hear the drums beating. Then all of a sudden, BEEP! The popcorn is done. You smell the the buttery saltyness waifting through the room. Then as you open the bag you start to take out the squeky, salty, buttery, butter yellow, dis mantling popcorn. and put the soft puffy popcorn in your mouth. And let it melt. "WOWIE" thats good stuff!

Figure 5.4 Sensory walk sample

	8/27/08 (5 senses)
Sight	• I saw a spider web dangeling in the breeze.
Sight	• I saw an ant hole with ant scurrying away from danger.
Hear	• I heard thousands of roaring cars zooming across t highway.
Sight	• I saw a tiger statue standing with so much pride he must be the king of tigers.
touch	• I felt a powerfull gust of wind.
Hear	• Birds were were chirping more beutiful then I ever heard.

Recognize Craft and Vocabulary Development • 151

As a wrap-up to each activity, my students write about each of the experiences. After becoming aware of the sensory details around them, the opportunity to describe the actual results solidifies the importance of the sensory images in reading. Any time a teacher can model a lesson with a mentor text, the more opportunities the students have to grasp the concept.

Graphic Organizers for Modeled and Intendant Reading

Sensory images bring reading to life and, as I stated earlier, strong sensory images draw the reader into the text, so much that they become a part of it through visualization. I would like to provide you with the following organizers (Table 5.2; Figures 5.5–5.6) that are designed to help students recognize and note sensory images as they read. Each organizer can be paired with one of the mentor texts in the list above for a read-aloud, with a poem, a chapter book, or a text a student has selected for independent reading.

Table 5.2 Visualizing 3-Column Chart

WORD OR PHRASE	I VISUALIZE ...	DEEPENED MY UNDERSTANDING BECAUSE ...

Figure 5.5 Graphic organizer for visualizing

In My Mind's Eye

Directions:
Write words or phrases from your reading in or around the thought bubble, then respond to the writing stem below.

This visualization helped me understand _____

_____
_____
_____
_____
_____
_____
_____
_____

Figure 5.6 Graphic organizer for mind scenes

Between the Scenes

Directions:
Good readers create "mind pictures" or images that go beyond the text. In the boxes below, sketch to fill in the missing information from today's reading. Then beside each sketch explain how these images helped you understand more deeply.

Vivid Verbs

Verbs are important to a text because if a verb is missing there won't be a sentence! Verbs serve several purposes:

- they make a statement;
- they ask questions;
- they give a command; and
- they express a state of being.

The more powerful or precise the verb, the more recognizable they are to the reader. Tom Romano tells us that, "verbs eliminate wasted energy and verbiage. Active verbs move readers across the white space." When students are reading, they need to notice the tense of the verb as well as the "strength" of the verb the author chose. Why? Because the *tense* provides evidence of when the story took place (past, present, future) and that is important for understanding. The *strength* of the verbs keeps the story moving and shows the passion the author has for the story either directly in an opinion or indirectly through the thoughts and actions of a character. An organizational chart like the one below (Table 5.3) helps students track the verb tenses during a teacher's read-aloud and then in their own independent reading. One of the best mentor texts that I have found, that not only teaches the basics of what verbs are but grabs the attention of all students, is *It's Hard to Be a Verb!* by Julia Cook.

Table 5.3 Verb Tenses

PRESENT	PAST	PAST PARTICIPLE*	PRESENT PARTICIPLE
laugh	*laughed*	*laughed*	*laughing*

* Uses helping verbs: has, have, or had.

Strong Verbs

Once students recognize what a verb is, its purpose and tense, they can begin to identify the use of strong verbs in the texts they are reading. This is an important craft skill at all grades. The verbs *to be* and *to have* are the most commonly used verbs in the English language. The problem is that the habitual use of *be* and *have* can make the text being read dull and boring. We want students to recognize the stronger verbs that not only add pizzazz to what they are reading but again cross over to the writing curriculum because we want students to add this pizzazz to their writing as well. When students look closely at what they are reading and recognize and note "what is good", including strong verbs, they are connecting to what they are reading. At the same time they are adding writing tools to their "tool belts." I have found that using a T-chart that provides a place for students to document strong verbs and then think "backwards" a bit and recall what the "weak verb" option could have been is an excellent tool to promote the purpose and importance of the strong verb.

Let's look at one of my favorite books for teaching a strong verb lesson, *Brave Irene* by William Steig. This book is a lengthier mentor text with numerous strong verbs, so the lesson usually takes several days to complete. The student sample on p. 157 (Figure 5.8) shows two days of modeling the text. The strong verbs found during the read-aloud were recorded on the left and the weak verbs that *could have* been used instead are recorded on the right side of the chart. The weak verbs are typically the ones students want to use in their own writing and this recognition of what is weak carries over to the importance of having several strong verb examples in their own writing.

Figure 5.7   Mentor texts for teaching strong verbs

- *Railroad John and the Red Rock Run* by Tony Crunk
- *The Everglades* by Jean Craighead George
- *Twilight Comes Twice* by Ralph Fletcher
- *Stellaluna* by Janell Cannon
- *Old Black Fly* by Jim Aylesworth

Figure 5.8 Student sample of strong verbs

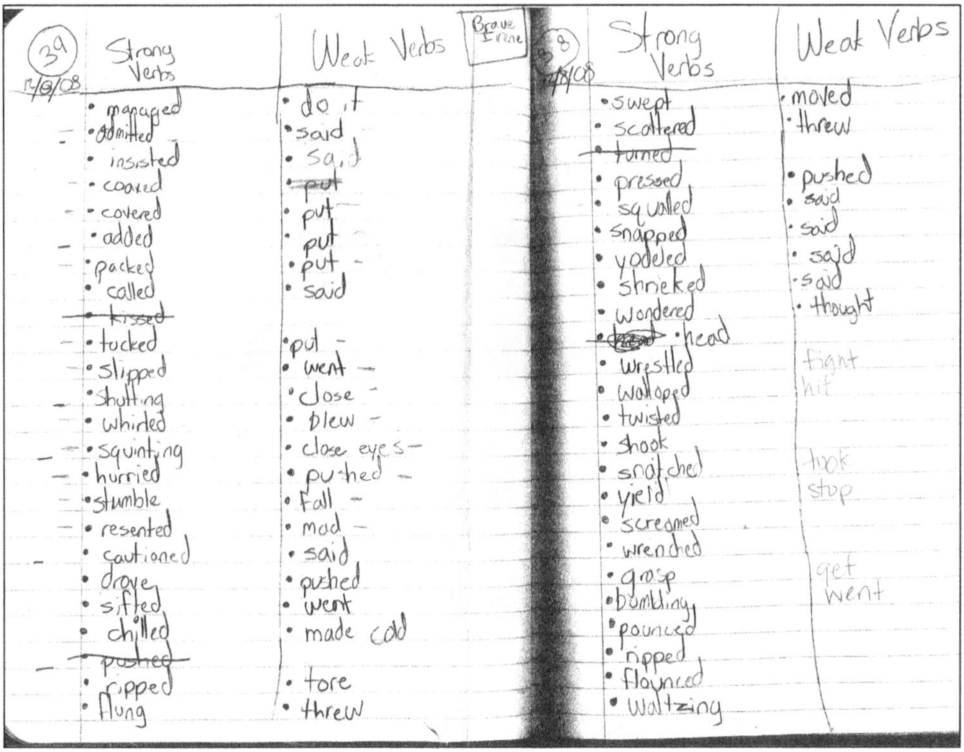

Similes

A simile compares two things using the words "like" or "as". Students love creating their own similes as well as locating them during reading. I keep a simple anchor chart in the room labeled SIMILES, and as students locate a simile during independent reading, they write it on a sticky note and attach it to the anchor chart. I also want students to recognize similes during my read-aloud time so sticky notes and pens are always available then as well.

I have been known to go a step further when teaching students to recognize similes. I find students grasp the purpose of similes more clearly when they categorize them as well. Since this craft example typically focuses on the senses, I divide my anchor chart into six sections. Each section is labeled with one of the *senses* and I add a section for *other* as well. When a student finds a simile for the sense of hearing, it is written on a sticky note and placed under the column for sound. The same routine applies to all of the senses. The other column generally refers to the feelings being projected through the use of a simile. It is important these are categorized as well. Table 5.4 is an example of a possible anchor chart.

Table 5.4 Categorizing Similes

SIGHT	HEARING	SMELL	TASTE	TOUCH	OTHER
The new baby looked as cute as a button in her new pajamas	The house was as quiet as a mouse when everyone was asleep	The glorious scent of the lavender smelled as sweet as Rachel's childhood memories	The apple pie tasted like heaven to the hungry family	When Joe rubbed the bark, it felt as rough as sandpaper	When she won the reading award, she felt as proud as a peacock

All about Similes

After students have an understanding of how to define, recognize, and categorize similes in their independent reading as well as during a read-aloud, it is important for them to craft their own original similes. Recognition of a skill is important, but being able to use that skill independently defines deeper understanding. (See Table 5.5.)

Idioms

An idiom is a phrase that has a meaning different from the dictionary definition. This craft skill begs for the opportunity for students to make an inference. Students use background knowledge in order to infer the literal meaning using textual evidence to recognize the idiomatic meaning of the expression. No idiom lesson is complete without an Amelia Bedelia book in hand. This delightful set of books, originally written by Peggy Parish, and then, after her death in the late 1980s, by her nephew Herman Parish, are an excellent resource for teaching. With a basket of books and the following organizer in hand, my students are ready to become idiom sleuths. (See Table 5.6.)

Table 5.5 All About Similes

ALL ABOUT SIMILES	
Comparing using "like" or "as"	
Simile:	
Write a sentence using the simile:	
Illustrate the two things you are comparing:	
I am writing about:	I compared it to:
Explain your comparison:	
Name:	Date:

Table 5.6 Recognizing Moments of Craft

IDIOM:	WHAT AMELIA LITERALLY DOES	WHAT THE IDIOM REALLY MEANS
"Oh, go fly a kite!"	Amelia went outside and flew a kite.	Go away and leave me alone.
A patient tells Amelia she "caught a bug."	Amelia tells the patient to let it go.	The patient was sick.

All about Idioms (Table 5.7) is an organizer that can be used with any text that includes examples of idioms. Students draw the two types of meaning as well as provide both types of meaning: literal and idiomatic. Each type of meaning requires a careful look for recognition of background knowledge for an inferred response.

Some additional "tried and true" activities that will ensure students recognize idioms in their reading, as well as the use of them in their writing, are:

1. Silly Stories

In this activity, students make up short stories using the silly meanings of idioms. These stories are always a hit with students and make them think about the true meanings of the idioms in order for the story to make sense. Figure 5.9 is an example.

2. Digging Dialogue

In this activity, students make up dialogue between two characters that involves a literal misinterpretation of one or more idioms. Listening to students share these masterpieces is a sure-fire way to build excitement and laughter in a lesson. Figure 5.10 is an example I wrote and use with students.

Table 5.7 All About Idioms

ALL ABOUT IDIOMS	
Idiom example:	
Idiomatic definition:	
Literal definition:	
Illustration of each definition:	
Idiomatic:	Literal:
Sentence using the idiom:	
Name:	Date:

Figure 5.9 Sample short story using idioms

> One day I watched a cool movie and just *cracked up*. As a matter of fact I was *in stitches* all night long. My sister was *all ears* when I told her about the movie. But the confused look she had on her face told me it was *over her head*.

Figure 5.10 Sample dialogue with misinterpreted idioms

> Sally: "Wow my report just *went down the drain*."
> Ralph: "Oh no, do you need some help retrieving it?"
> Sally: "I didn't mean to *throw you a curve* with that comment."
> Ralph: "I am pretty good at softball so go ahead . . . but inside the building may not be a good idea."
> Sally: "I can tell this conversation is *as clear as a bell* to you."
> Ralph: "The bell? OK, I am off to class now."

3. Idiom Charades

Students enjoy clowning around, and as long as it is centered on a learning opportunity, I am all for it. When playing this kind of charades, each student is given a card with an idiom written on it. A list of the idioms I have written on the cards is also displayed at the front of the room to be used as a reference so that authentic guesses can be made. One student stands at the front of the room, reads the idiom example on the card and acts out the literal meaning of the idiom. Using dialogue to convey the point is also helpful with this activity. For example, if a student draws the card needle in a haystack, they may get down on the floor, move their hands in a way that suggests they are searching and say, "I will never find that earring." Students would then decide which idiom is being acted out.

Figure 5.11 shows a few of the idioms that are on the list in the classroom as well as written on the cards.

4. Idiomnary

A variation of the charades activity which is played much like Pictionary where teams are selected but, unlike charades where the students act out the literal meaning of the idiom, a sketch of the figurative example is drawn. For example, if a student selects a card with the idiom *apple of my eye*, written on it, they may draw a character face that has, in place of eyes, mini apples. The team player who guesses the idiom example that was drawn, as well as verbally providing the literal meaning correctly, receives a point for their team. I even use the sand timer from an old Pictionary game for this activity.

Figure 5.11 Idioms listed in the classroom

IDIOMS	
Take the cake	Needle in a haystack
Throw a curve	Cool as a cucumber
Down the drain	Piece of cake
On the double	Going bananas
Clear as a bell	For the birds
Down in the dumps	Bend over backwards
Drive you crazy	Call the shots
Not your cup of tea	Apple of my eye
Off the wall	

Hyperbole

A hyperbole is an extravagant exaggeration, usually in the form of bragging, that is not meant to be taken literally. Bragging was a common form of entertainment in the 1800s and was not intended to be factual. This form of communication was a humorous way, used by settlers, to adapt to the hardship of the tough environment and lifestyle they had to endure. This is an important point to make with English language learners. I have seen many confused looks among my ELL students when the class comes across an example of hyperbole in their reading. In order to minimalize this confusion, we always take the time to stop, recognize, and clarify the actual meaning of the phrases. An anchor chart of examples is clearly displayed for everyone to see and refer to (Figure 5.12).

Tying in the traditional literature of tall tales is a natural way for students to recognize the use of hyperbole. Some examples of traditional tall tale titles that I use for instruction are written by my favorite author, Steven Kellogg. There are numerous tall tale titles as well as other genre opportunities for teaching hyperbole and I have listed several of them in Figure 5.13.

Figure 5.12 Hyperbole examples

- My backpack *weighs a ton*.
- I felt like I *hadn't eaten in years*.
- The pile of garbage *reached the sky*.
- The siren could be *heard around the world*.
- The test was *never ending*.
- My mom *told me a million times* not to slam the door.
- I am so hungry I could *eat a horse*.
- This class is *taking forever*.

Figure 5.13 Tall tales by Steven Kellogg

- *Paul Bunyan*
- *Pecos Bill*
- *Babe and the Blue Ox*
- *Johnny Appleseed*

1. Hyperbole Mini-Posters

For this activity, students are given a piece of 9" x 12" construction paper and art materials. These materials include markers, index cards, rulers, and pictures from magazines or catalogues. At the bottom of the poster, a hyperbole example is written on the index card or a sentence strip and glued either to the top or bottom of the poster. Students have the option of illustrating the hyperbole or finding pictures that closely relate to the hyperbole and adding details to help bring the hyperbole to life. I make sure that each student has selected a different hyperbole to illustrate. Students can select an example from the anchor chart in the classroom or write their own. After the front of the poster has been assembled, students write the literal meaning of the hyperbole on the back of the poster. A variation of this activity is for students to divide the construction paper into quarters, so that there are four squares, and a different hyperbole example is written in each section along with an illustration. These posters can be displayed on a bulletin board and then compiled into a class book later.

A chart that provides students with a little practice in writing hyperboles is found in Figure 5.14 below. I also vary the chart a bit so that students can document hyperboles that they find in their independent reading. This variation is found in Figure 5.15.

Figure 5.14 Practice writing hyperboles

LET'S WRITE HYPERBOLES	
What is your subject?	
What is the hyperbole that you will compare your subject to?	
Write a sentence using your hyperbole:	
Illustrate your sentence:	
Name:	Date:

2. Hyperbole Poems

Students enjoy writing poems, and when the opportunity to get a "bit silly with a purpose" is given, the creativity flows. For the hyperbole poems, the first goal is for students to recognize the figurative language as well as the literary devices found in poems that we read together in class. The next goal is for students to write their own poems using several hyperbole examples. These poems may or may not rhyme and that is OK. Because of the nature of the hyperbole, the poems will rarely make complete sense and they will be silly, but that is also OK. The following is an example poem written by

Figure 5.15 Hyperboles students find in their reading

LET'S READ HYPERBOLES	
Hyperbole example found in the text:	
Illustrate the text sample:	
Describe the author's purpose for the hyperbole:	
Rewrite the text example using a different hyperbole:	
Name:	Date:

Lil Pluta. It is a humorous poem that helps students recognize the use of hyperbole as well as define the purpose of these exaggerations, which is to entertain.

Hyperbole Café by Lil Pluta

Welcome to our restaurant.
Where everything's gigantic.
A hundred waiters hold one dish.
Our kitchen can get frantic
Our soup is deeper than the sea.
Our noodles stretch a mile.
The bread is longer than a train.
It's sure to make you smile.
We pile our peas up mountain high.
One cookie hides the moon.
We pour our iced tea into boats.
We hope you'll visit soon.

Figure 5.16 shows additional mentor texts I use when teaching hyperbole.

Figure 5.16 *Additional mentor texts for teaching hyperbole*

Piggie Pie by Margie Palatini

Cloudy with a Chance of Meatballs by Judi Barrett

Dust Devil by Anne Isaacs (tall tale)

Swamp Angel by Anne Isaacs

Hyperbole and a Half by Allie Brosh

Thunder Rose by Jerdine Nolen (tall tale)

Big Jabe by Jerdine Nolen (tall tale)

Fin Throws a Fit by David Elliott

Could be Worse! by James Stevenson

A Million Fish . . . More or Less by Patricia McKissack

John Henry by Julius Lester (tall tale)

Alexander and the Terrible, Horrible, No Good, Very Bad Day by Judith Viorst

---

Personification

When writers give human characteristics or qualities (actions or feelings) to inanimate objects or ideas, we call this personification. The use of the word "person" within the spelling of this craft skill is always a helpful reminder of the definition. During a read-aloud, an anchor chart is displayed to collect examples from the text. Teachers understand that the first step to understanding is for students to (1) recognize with assistance, (2) recognize without assistance and then (3) apply in their writing.

I spend a good amount of time allowing students to recognize personification in texts that I read aloud, and then after I see, through active participation in this assisted recognition, that students can recognize the personification, they are asked to independently complete a chart, like the one in Table 5.8, on a smaller scale in their notebooks or a graphic organizer. Finally, personification is added to our revising toolbox and students are asked to use it, when applicable, in writer's workshops as well as when summarizing a text.

Table 5.8 Recognizing Personification

INANIMATE OBJECT	HUMAN QUALITY	LITERAL MEANING
The ancient car	groaned into third gear.	The car had a difficult time switching gears.
The tropical storm	slept for two days.	The storm went away for two days.
The trees	shivered in the wind.	The cold wind blew the trees.

Activities and Mentor Texts for Teaching Audible Craft

Alliteration

Alliteration is the repetition of initial *sounds* in consecutive words. I stress the word sounds because often students think that alliteration is simply the repetition of letters, and that is not the case. For example, *fish* and *physics* alliterate because both words make the same consonant sound (f). The purpose of alliteration is to create rhythm and word play as well as create an auditory interest in the reader. It is interesting to students when teachers point out how advertisements and name brands often use alliteration to catch the buyer's attention. A few examples are: Best Buy, Krispy Kreme, and PayPal. I also point out alliterative character names that we find in our reading. As readers we are inferring that the author used this technique on purpose to help readers remember the name of the character. Challenge your students to recognize and note when characters or settings are brought to light with alliteration.

1. "I'm Going on a Trip"

Everyone loves the classic "I'm going on a bear hunt . . ." and for alliteration, I just change the words a bit. As I sit in front of the class, I begin my story with "I am going on a trip and I need to bring a suitcase". Students take turns making suggestions for what I need, making sure that the item begins with the letter "S". After several rounds with the letter "S", a student takes my place and begins the game with a different letter. As the students become more familiar with the initial consonant words, I change it up and begin my list of needs with a consonant blend: *gl, sw, wh, tr*, etc.

2. Letter/Sound Web

The classic web is a great tool to focus on initial sounds. For this activity, students close their eyes and select a letter or consonant blend from a basket. The choice they draw is then written in the middle of a circle in their reader's notebooks. I set the timer for 2 minutes and have the students brainstorm words that have the same initial sound. After the web is complete, students write a tongue-twister using as many of the words from their web as they can. To adapt this to reading, as students read in their chapter books for independent reading, higher level words are collected from a letter or initial sound that the student chooses. After a couple of days of reading and collecting, the same process for writing a tongue-twister is used, except this time the words are focused around the text that is being read. Figure 5.17 shows sample mentor texts with alliteration examples.

Figure 5.17   Mentor texts for alliteration

> *The Absolutely Awful Alphabet* by Mordicai Gerstein
>
> *Some Smug Slug* by Pamela Duncan Edwards
>
> *A My Name is ALICE* by Jane Bayer
>
> *Princess Pigtoria and the Pea* by Pamela Duncan Edwards
>
> *Bootsie Barker Bites* by Barbara Botner
>
> * Most poetry written by Shel Silverstein or Jack Prelutsky

Assonance

Unlike alliteration where the initial sound is stressed, assonance is the internal repetition of vowel sounds in words that are close together. An example would be, "Do you like blue?" Writers use it to create internal rhyme that makes the words flow together, and can help make the phrases more memorable. This device can be found in poems and songs. Assonance is also known as the "slant rhyme". I find that the best way to study assonance is through poetry. An organizer below is an excellent tool for students to use to locate as well as create assonance in their reading and writing. I find that, even with my fourth graders, this craft skill can be a bit tricky. The fact that the sounds are not initial, rather embedded in the word, requires more

Figure 5.18 Mentor texts to help teach assonance

> *BIG Chickens* by Leslie Helakoski
>
> *Beetle Bop* by Denise Fleming
>
> *Superhero ABC* by Bob McLeod
>
> *Duck in the Truck* by Jez Alborough
>
> *Tumble Bumble* by Felicia Bond
>
> *Chicka Chicka 123* by Bill Martin Jr.
>
> *All You Need for a Snowman* by Alice Schertle

thought and recognition. By the way, the word assonance has assonance because of the sound the two 'a's make. Figure 5.18 shows sample mentor texts with assonance examples.

Onomatopoeia

Sizzle, snap, crack and pop! Onomatopoeia is a word or a group of words that imitate a sound. Often these examples are written in capitals to emphasize the sound imitated. If you ever read the Superman comics, you will remember that words such as POW! or BAM! were often represented through onomatopoeia. In his poem, *The Bells*, Edgar Allen Poe wrote about the "tintinnabulation" of the bells. This completely made-up word helps the reader "hear" the sounds an object is making, and that is the main purpose of the onomatopoeia, to bring words to life for the reader. No one can deny that students like to make noises, and when teaching them about this form of craft, students rise to the occasion. There are several activities that I have found to be successful with either introducing or reinforcing this skill.

1. Sound Range Charts

Recognizing onomatopoeia is important, but so is recognizing the noise range of the words. As my students are collecting onomatopoeia from an assortment of texts, I provide a "range chart" like the one in Figure 5.19. As you can see from the example, the louder sound words go at the top of the chart, the softer ones at the bottom, and those in between go in the middle. It is a simple

Figure 5.19 Range chart

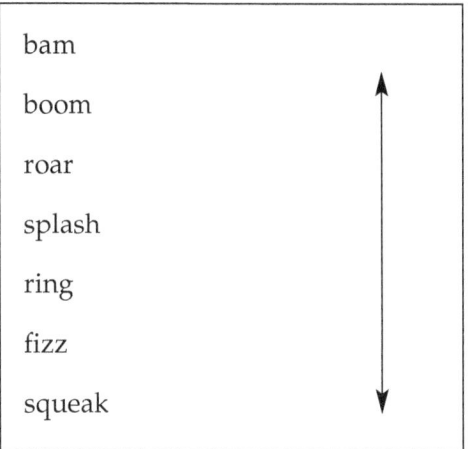

Figure 5.20 T-chart variation on the range chart

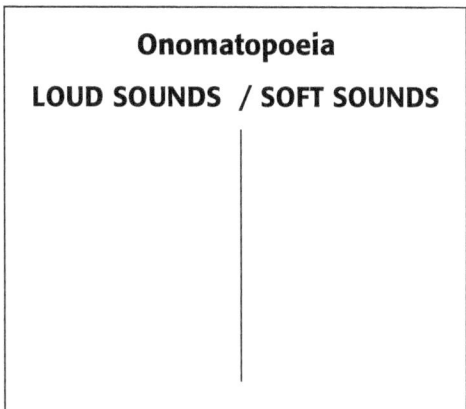

yet effective way to ensure that students use the clues within the text to determine how "loud" the word is or how soft. This is also helpful when students use onomatopoeia in their own writing. The last thing I want is for students to begin randomly adding sound words just for the sake of adding them. Onomatopoeia has a purpose, and that is to grab the attention of the reader. A variation of the range chart is for students to record the sound levels in the same way but use a T-chart instead (Figure 5.20).

2. Cartoon/Comic Creations

Students love cartoons and action. This activity promises to make them smile, and to help with recognition as well as creating some onomatopoeia fun. After the onomatopoeia detective activity has been completed and several mentor texts containing these sound word examples have been read, students can now go to the next level of understanding—writing with the craft skill. For this exploration, students brainstorm examples of onomatopoeia in cartoons or movies that they have watched. I like to show a variety of YouTube student-friendly video clips to help with the brainstorming. After a list of words have been generated on an anchor chart, students find a partner and together create an action-packed cartoon script to share with the class. Remind the groups that the more sound the better. A variation of this activity is to ask the pairs of students to write a 6-scene comic strip using as many of the onomatopoeia words from the chart, or any that come to mind while writing the comic. A simple row of five to six boxes, or five or six index cards, can be used for this activity (Figure 5.21).

Figure 5.21 Row of boxes for comic creations

☐ ☐ ☐ ☐ ☐

3. Noisy Homework

It is time for students to watch a little TV . . . for homework! With an onomatopoeia chart and a couple of nights documenting the sound words that were heard while watching TV, students have a clearer sense of how prevalent sounds are in our everyday lives. I am always amazed at the number of words that are collected on an anchor chart after this homework assignment. With the popularity of video games, I have altered my homework guidelines to include the sounds heard from games as well. Figure 5.22 is an example of the homework assignment guidelines that are sent home.

Figure 5.22 Homework guidelines

> Dear Parents,
>
> In class we are studying many examples of the craft of language that writers use and readers need to recognize. One in particular is onomatopoeia. Onomatopocia is a group of words that imitate a sound. For the next couple for nights, students are asked to record any *sound* words that are heard while watching television or even playing their favorite video games. The spelling of these words will be creative and made up, and that is OK. The point is to recognize this strategy.
>
> Thank you,
>
> _____
>
> **Word List**

Tying in Vivid Vocabulary

Emphasizing words not only applies to the craft of language but also supports vocabulary development. Janet Allen reminds us that vocabulary instruction that "makes words meaningful, memorable, and useful begins with shared experiences." Our goal, as teachers, is to motivate students to think about words and respect the word choices made by writers. In turn, we want students to become aware of their own word choices and why they made them. It is also important for students to realize that readers must understand the words in a text in order to comprehend what is being read. Studying vocabulary words before, during, and after reading helps develop schema and understanding.

This section of the chapter will not only be a variety of activities much like the ones for the language of craft, but also gives six graphic organizers that are at the top of my list for effectiveness.

1. Four Fold

Students fold their papers into rows of four sections each. The number of rows can relate to the number of words studied. In the first section, the students write the word. In the second section the students write the definition in their own words. The third section is a favorite for my students, because they get the chance to draw a picture or a symbol that represents the word. Finally, in section four, a sentence is written that demonstrates the understanding of the word definition. During independent reading, students collect higher level words that they notice and jot them down in their reader's notebooks. I ask for my students to code the words with a ? if further study is required (using the chart below and organizers at the end of this chapter) and a ♥ if they know what the word means, and recognize that it is one that should be used in writing. Table 5.9 shows the chart.

Table 5.9 Four Fold Chart

WORD	DEFINITION	PICTURE	SENTENCE
embedded			
distinguish			
frolic			

2. Interview with a Word

Students choose a vocabulary word that was either collected during independent reading or provided by the teacher. The goal is for students to imagine that they are the word and must answer interview-type questions to demonstrate their overall knowledge of the word. This activity makes an excellent class-made word workbook. (See Figure 5.23).

Figure 5.23 Interview with a word

I am (vocabulary word) _____

My part of speech is _____

1. What words mean the same as you?
2. What makes you happy?
3. Who or what is your best friend?
4. What do you dislike the most?
5. If you could give anyone advice, who would you give it to and what would you say?

_____
_____
_____
_____

6. Draw a self-portrait of yourself.

3. Quick Draw

This activity does not have to be competitive, but it can be. The class is broken up into teams. Each team representative is shown a vocabulary word. Since I also teach Social Studies, I use content area vocabulary for this activity. It can be in the introduction of vocabulary in a chapter or unit that is about to be studied or as a review of a chapter or unit that has already been studied. The goal is to see how quickly students can convey the meaning of the word without using words. This activity works especially well with words describing visual concepts, as many geography words do. The first team to guess what the vocabulary word is gets a point. This activity can be made more difficult by asking the team members not only to guess which vocabulary word is being drawn, but to provide the definition of the word as well.

4. Linear Arrays

Linear arrays are used to extend vocabulary recognition by asking students to extend their understanding of selected words (again from my Social Studies units). By using opposites at each end of the array, students add words that are in between. The vocabulary word is written in the first box, the antonym of the word in the last box. The words "in between" are written in the circles. Teachers can start off with one circle, then add more as students become better word sleuths. A variation of this activity is, instead of students writing only the words in the array, to have them find pictures or images of the word and cut and paste them within the shapes as well. See Figure 5.24.

Figure 5.24 Linear array

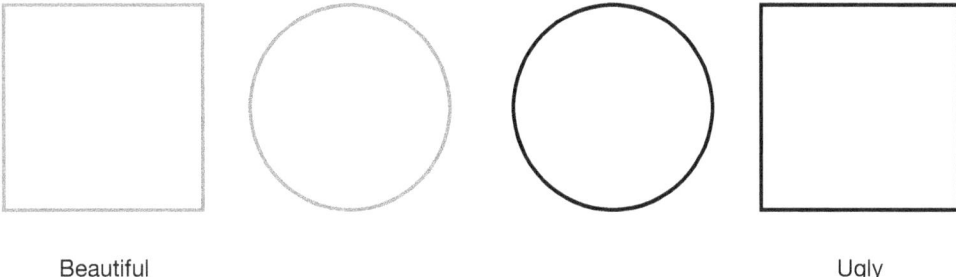

Beautiful   Ugly

5. Own Don't Rent

One problem that students seem to have is learning the vocabulary words, not just memorizing them. I found that if students write the definition of words in their *own* words, they remember, long term, what the definitions are. Because I also feel that using a dictionary and locating definitions the "good old fashioned way" is still important, we call this "renting" the words in my classroom. A simple chart helps students with this concept. See the student sample in Figure 5.25.

6. Zap It

This activity is always a hit with students, and it requires little preparation. All you need is a plastic jar and Popsicle sticks. A label is created for the front of the jar that says "ZAP IT!"

The activity is played in teams. Two players draw a stick from the jar that has a content area vocabulary word written on the bottom of it, so that students cannot see what word is being selected. In order to keep the stick for their team, the definition of the word on the stick must quickly and correctly be written on the board. The first player to do this gets to keep the stick. Now, if a Popsicle stick is pulled from the jar with the words Zap It! written on it, all of the sticks that the team has earned must go back in the jar. After several rounds have been played, the team with the most number of sticks wins!

Figure 5.25 Student sample of rent vs. own

Paragraph 3

Rent	Own
A female praying mantis sits motionless in a bush.	A female praying mantis sit movingless on some bush branches.
Her thin, green body blends in with the leaves around her.	Her green, thin body camoflouges with the bush leaves around her.
It is not aware of the killer on the branches below it.	The large cricket nibbles on the leaves above the killer below it, not aware of the killer.
The praying mantis lashes out with her front legs.	The praying mantis suddenly lurches at the cricket using her front legs.
Rows of sharp spikes on her front legs spear the cricket.	Her sharp, spikey legs spear the large cricket in front of her.
As fierce as praying mantises are, they are not without enemies.	Praying mantises, of course, aren't fierce with no enemies.
The giant hornet is a mantis killer.	An Asian giant hornet is one of the praying mantis' enemies.

NW.s

17.

Recognize Craft and Vocabulary Development • 177

Graphic Organizers to Aid Vocabulary Study

Figure 5.26 Word chart

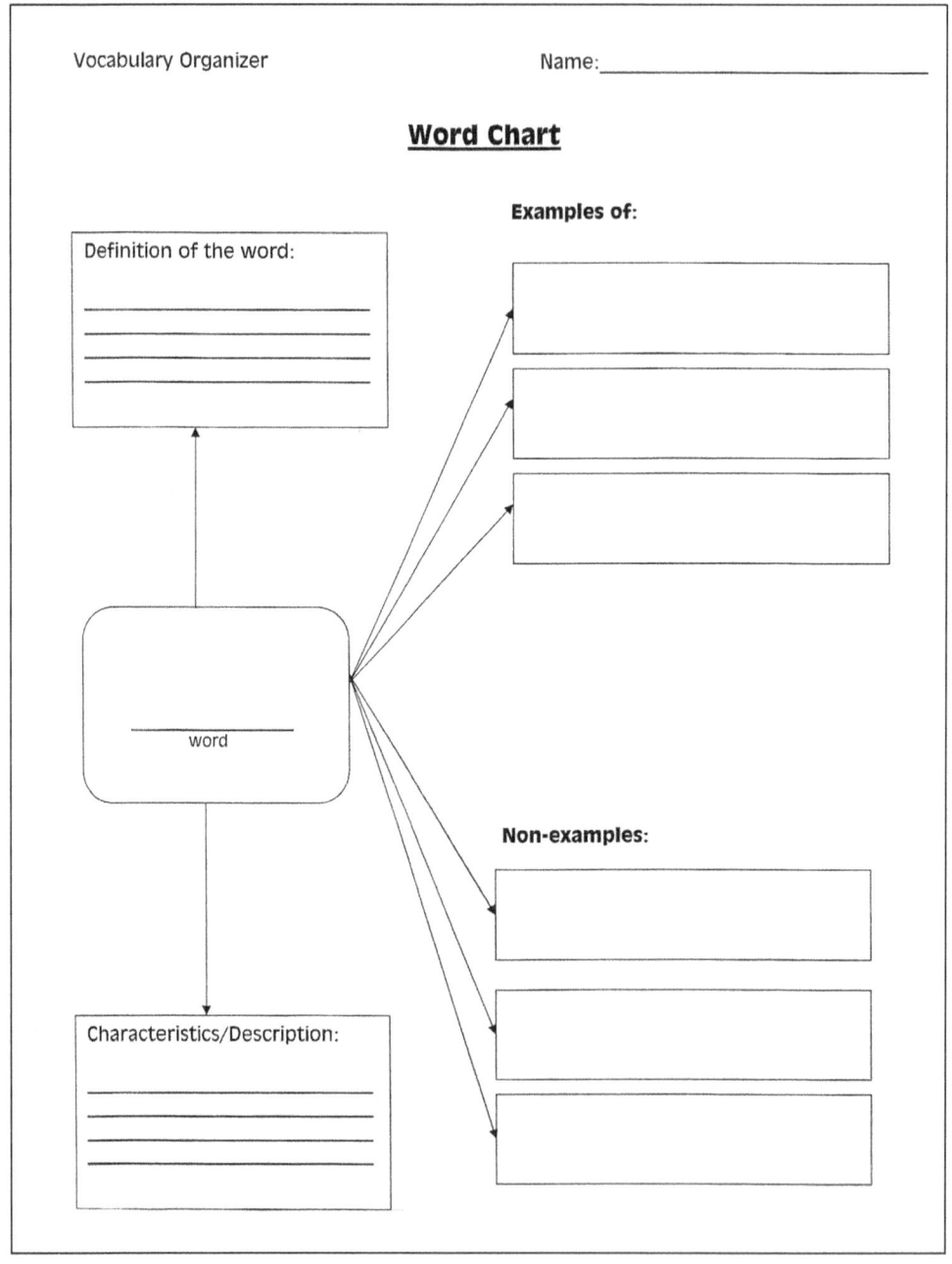

Figure 5.27 Word map

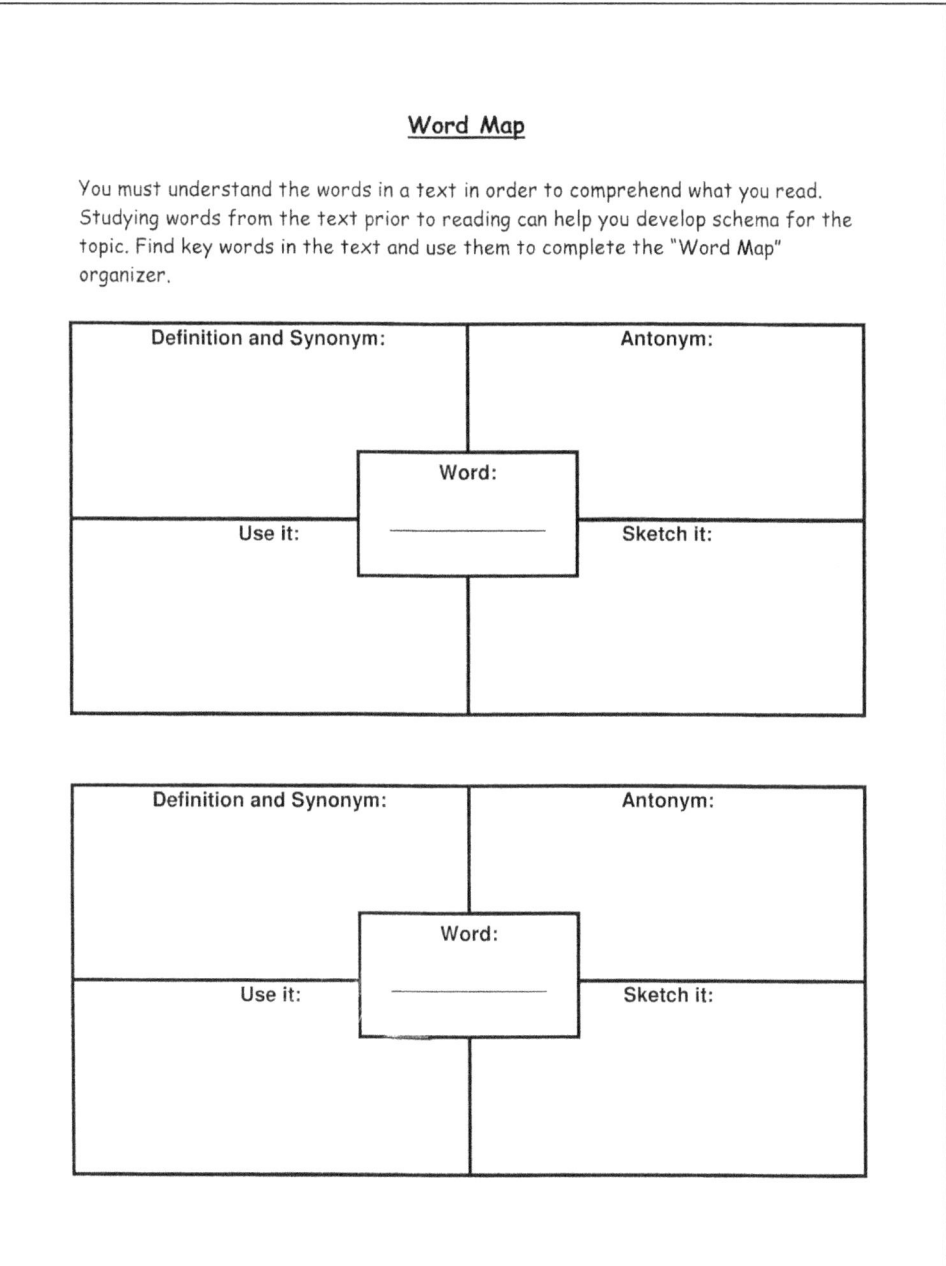

Figure 5.28 Mini dictionary

Vocabulary Organizer
Mini Dictionary

Name:_____

synonym

antonym

illustration

Word Meaning:_____

Sentence:_____

synonym

antonym

illustration

Word Meaning:_____

Sentence:_____

Figure 5.29 Word connections

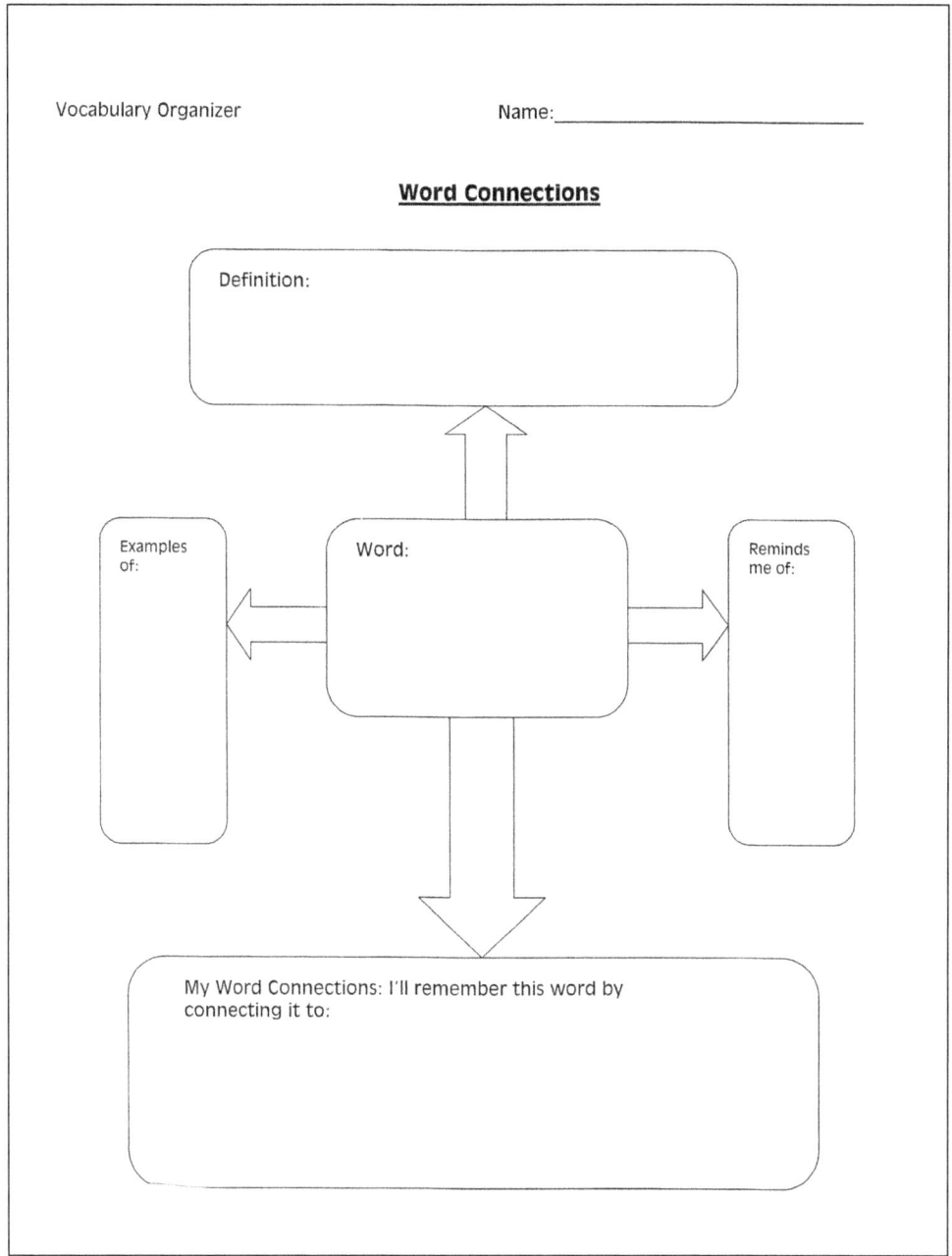

Figure 5.30 Word descriptions

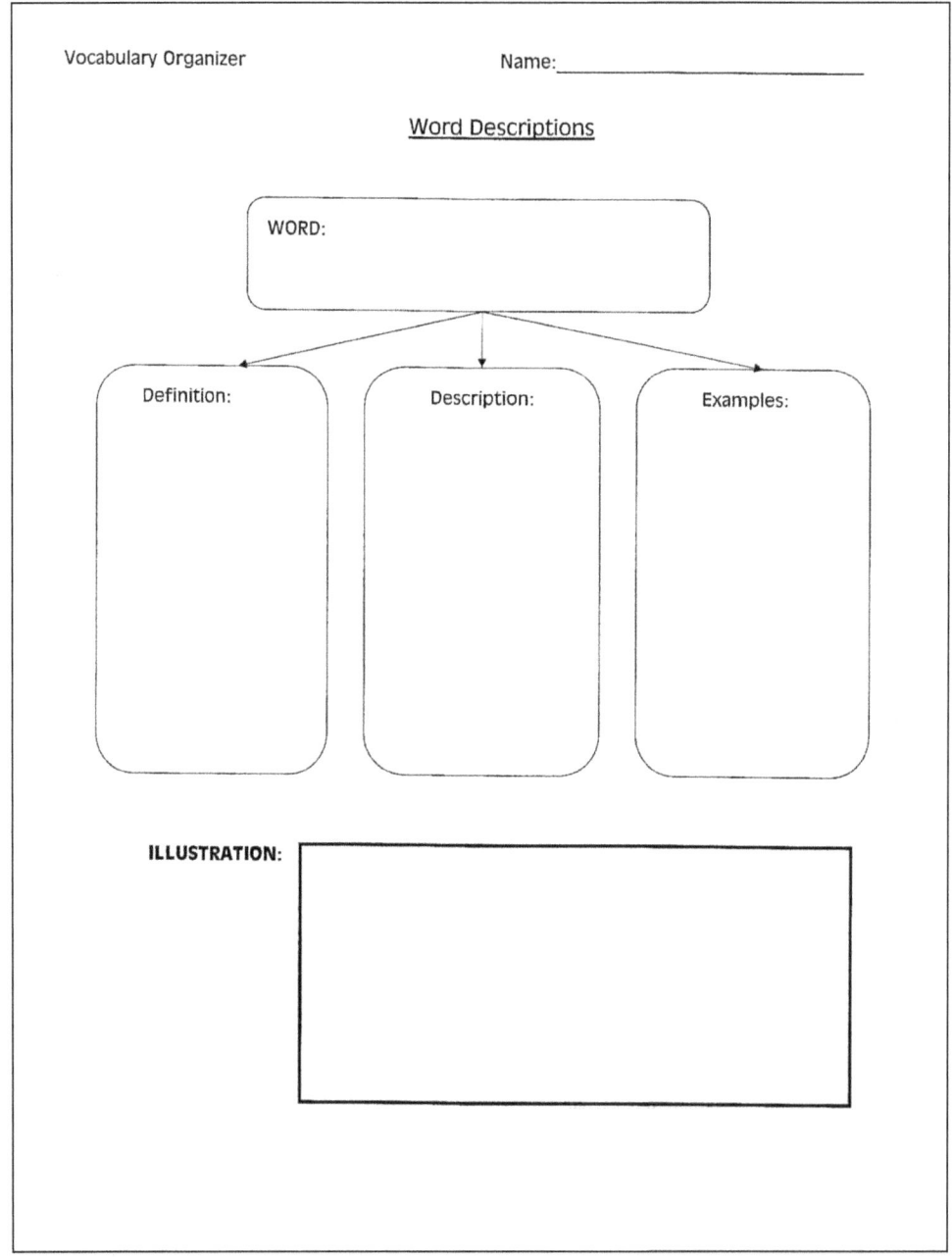

Figure 5.31 Word pyramid

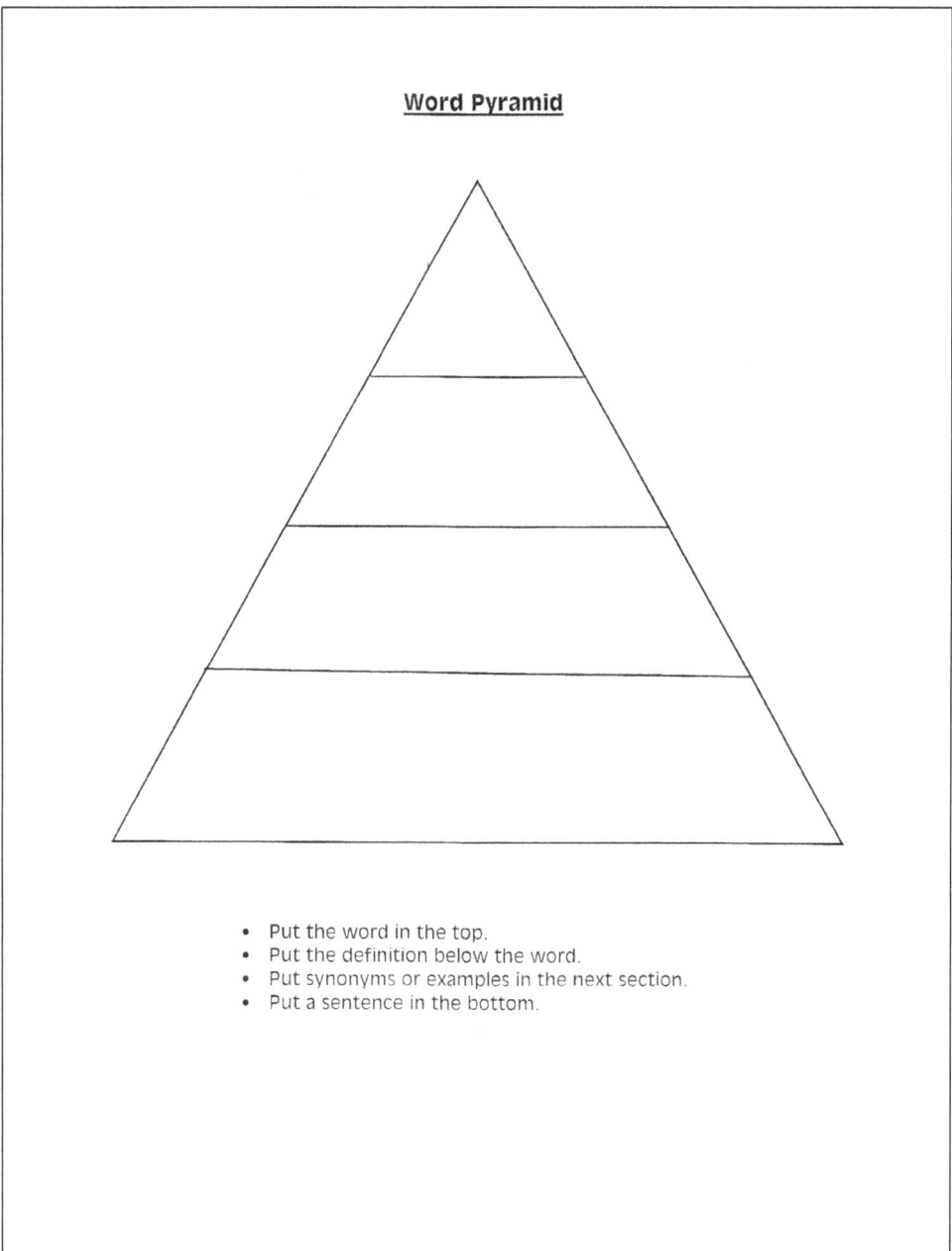

Monitoring the Mood and Tone

Tone and mood are literary elements that are integrated into pieces of writing. Tone is the author's attitude towards the audience, the subject, or the characters. Tone is determined by *description* or *dialogue*. Mood is the feeling that the reader gets from the story. Mood is determined by *setting* or *atmosphere*. Authors set a tone or mood in literature by conveying an emotion or emotions through words. Identifying the tone and mood in literature is important to help readers understand what the author is trying to say. Let's look at the following descriptions (Figures 5.32 and 5.33) and see the differences between the two elements.

Figure 5.32 Description of tone

Some Adjectives to Describe TONE

formal, informal, inspiring, serious, humorous, amused, angry, playful, neutral, satirical, gloomy, conciliatory, sad, resigned, cheerful, ironic, clear, detailed, imploring, suspicious, witty . . .

Figure 5.33 Description of mood

Some Adjectives to Describe MOOD

fictional, imaginary, cozy, familiar, fanciful, idealistic, romantic, realistic, optimistic, pessimistic, gloomy, mournful, sorrowful, anxious, strained, nervous . . .

Passage Samples

Tone

The author's tone in this passage is inspiring. The descriptions play a major role in relaying the tone. Remember, tone is determined by description or dialogue. I wrote the passage in Figure 5.34, about my daughter, to show the class an example.

Figure 5.34 Tone passage

> Bella
>
> There is no one like you.
>
> There is no one **better or more brilliant**.
>
> There is **nothing you cannot do** because you are **unstoppable.**
>
> There **is no place you cannot go** because your **loving personality** is **always welcomed**.
>
> There is no one like you.

Mood

The mood of the following passage is cozy and familiar. As Christmas is one of my favorite holidays, I wrote this passage (Figure 5.35) to show how the atmosphere plays a role in the mood. Remember, mood is determined by the setting or atmosphere.

Figure 5.35 Mood passage

> **Christmas Eve**
>
> As the door swings open, in walk my **friends and family**. The **Christmas tree is lit** and the **presents are wrapped**. The **soft glow of candles** and the **warming fire** is peaceful. From outside, we can hear **carolers singing** Christmas songs and the **soft pitter-patter** of snow as it **falls gently** to the ground.

Mood Task Cards

The following task cards (Figure 5.36) can be used in a reading station, after a read-aloud, or put on labels and used for a writing opportunity in the reader's notebooks.

Figure 5.36 Task cards

Task Card #1
How did you feel while reading this story? Why did you feel this way?

Task Card #2
What do you remember most about the story? What words did the author use to help you remember?

Task Card #3
What was the funniest, scariest, or strangest thing that happened during the story?

Task Card #4
How did the author make you feel the way you did when you read this story?

Task Card #5
What was the most exciting thing that happened in the story?

Identifying the Author's Tone or Mood

It is important for students to find evidence of the author's tone and mood in the word choice of the text they are reading. The graphic organizer in Table 5.10 provides students with a place to document this evidence while they are reading.

Table 5.10 Identifying the Author's Tone

Author's tone:	Specific words that the author used to convey the tone:
Author's mood:	Specific words that the author used to convey the mood:

Connecting with Illustrations

Illustrations add so much to a picture book. We often tell our students not to judge a book by its cover but, in reality, it is hard not to. Pictures can evoke emotions within the reader and help make connections. I have a basket of books in my class library filled with books that have illustrations that still take my breath away every time I read them to my students. Figure 5.37 shows a few of those titles.

Figure 5.37 Books with powerful illustrations

Rumpelstiltskin by Paul O. Zelinsky

Grandfather Twilight by Barbara Helen Burger

The Twelve Days of Christmas by Jan Brett

Zen Shorts by Jin J. Muth

Cinderella by K.Y. Craft

The Rainbabies by Laura Krauss Melmed

Owl Babies by Martin Waddell

King Bridgood's in the Bath by Audrey Wood

The Lion and the Mouse by Jerry Pinkney

Illustration Task Cards

In one of my reading stations, I place the basket of books mentioned above along with a set of task cards. Each task card is numbered and students respond in their reader's notebooks (Figure 5.38). I love using generic-type task cards because the questions on the cards stay the same, all the teacher has to do is change the book the students are focused on.

Figure 5.38 Illustration task cards

Card #1

Do you like the illustrations? Explain, in detail, why or why not.

Card #2

What, if anything, did the illustrations add to the text?

Card #3

What do you think the illustrator needed to know in order to illustrate the story?

Card #4

Would more illustrations help the reader understand the story? Why or why not?

Card #5

What connections did you make to the illustrations? Were the connections text to self, text to text, or text to world? Explain your answer.

Choice Board

R	E	A	D
Choose what you think is the most visual element of the text. Sketch or describe this visual. Then explain why you think it is important.	What are oral presentations? How does an oral presentation of a story get readers excited and engaged in the story?	What is the mood or tone of the story you are reading? Use evidence from the text to support your decision.	Select at least three similes and/or metaphors from the book that you are reading. Explain how these similes or metaphors helped you visualize the story.
Find five interesting words from the story you are reading. Write each word in an original sentence.	Find five examples of figurative language in the story that you are reading. Write the example, the type it is, and the meaning of the phrase.	Find five unknown words. Use context clues to determine the meaning of each word. Then look up each word in a dictionary and check your definitions.	Choose a scene from your book that contains visual elements. Explain your connection to this scene and how the visuals helped you make that connection.

Closing Thoughts

The magic of words has always appealed to me as both a reader and a writer. Identifying the craft and language an author uses helps me make deeper personal connections to the writing. Teachers want the same from their students. And because words are so relevant to the way our students speak and write, it is important that they are able to recognize and define the higher level vocabulary opportunities in a read-aloud by the teacher as well as in their own independent writing.

Chapter 6

Recognizing the Structural Elements of Prose, Poetry, and Drama

"A reader lives a thousand lives before he dies. The man who never reads lives only one."

George R.R. Martin

Standards RL.5 and RL.6

I Can Statements

- I can tell my teacher or friend about the different parts of poems and plays that I read.
- I can recognize that poems, drama, and prose use different structural elements.
- I can identify common structural elements of poems and dramas.
- I can refer to the structural elements of a poem when explaining their differences.
- I can compare and contrast the points of view from which different stories are narrated, including the difference between first and third person.
- I can identify basic points of view as first person and third person.
- I can compare the points of view in different stories.
- I can contrast the points of view in different stories.

Figure 6.1 Another look at my notes

Chapter 6: Crate #5—Pink

RL.4.5: Explain major differences between poems, prose, and refer to the structural elements of poems (verse, rhythm, meter) and drama (casts of characters, setting, descriptions, dialogue, stage directions) when writing or speaking about a text.

- Making connections to other texts (text to text connections)
- Author study
- Closer look at genres: prose, poetry, and drama
- Narrative structure vs. other genres (compare/contrast)
- Illustrations

RL.4.6: Compare and contrast the point of view from which different stories are narrated, including the difference between first- and third-person narrations.

- Point of view
- Effectiveness of choice between the two "views"
- Writing opportunity—change the point of view of the selection and compare how it affects the reader

---

Comparing Prose, Poetry, and Drama

Before the CCSS, the words prose and drama were not typically used to identify the precise type of literature we were reading. Of course we identified tall tales, poetry, historical fiction, etc., but until I studied further what texts, for example, came within the category of prose (personal narrative, speeches, broadcasts) I focused on simply categorizing our reading as fiction and non-fiction. The standards want teachers to compare genres, and looking closely at what falls within prose, poetry, and drama is a good place to start. In Chapter 3, I looked at an introduction to genres and how the different types could be taught throughout the year alongside the comprehension strategies. In this chapter, I want to look a little bit closer at what defines the three major categories: prose, poetry, and drama.

A Chart to Keep Focused

A simple anchor chart can help students identify the similarities (most of what we read) and the differences between these three types of texts that will be read and studied.

Table 6.1 Comparing Three Types of Texts

PROSE	POETRY	DRAMA
• Written in sentences, one after the other, called paragraphs • Regular writing (letters, journals, diaries, short stories, novels, certain poetry) • Organized in paragraphs or chapters • News or magazine articles (non-fiction prose)	• Many poems rhyme • Written in lines • Groups of lines are called stanzas or a verse • Has beats and rhythm (songs and chants)	• Tells a story • It is a play • Uses dialogue • Characters, setting, a plot • Entertaining • Begins with a cast of characters (play) • Stage directions

There are many different types of genre of literature. The chart below piggy-backs, or expands, the chart above. I keep both charts hanging on the wall for reference. Students also have minimized copies (85 percent fits well) in their reader's notebooks. Each of these genres fits within one of the categories of prose, poetry, and drama; most fit within prose.

Keeping Track of Reading Selections

Holding students accountable for reading different genres, while also giving them free choice, is an important element in the successful classroom. Even though I like to keep "all like curriculum" within units of study, that does not mean that the students are inhibited from also reading genres of their choice. The boys in my classroom eat up fantasy and historical fiction. So even if I am focusing my curriculum on poetry, the students celebrate the other genres they read either at home, in book clubs, or in their free time.

Table 6.2 A Closer Look at Different Genres

GENRE	DESCRIPTION
Drama	A written story meant to be acted out on stage.
Fable	A story meant to teach a useful lesson that often has animals that speak and act like humans.
Folk tale	A traditional story with a moral or lesson handed down by people of a region from one generation to the next.
Myth	An old story, handed down through time, that might tell about gods and heroes or explain events in nature.
Novel	A fictional story longer in text, that fills up a book.
Short story	A short work of fiction with a limited number of characters and usually a single plot.
Poetry	A short piece of writing often with rhyme and a particular rhythm.
Essay	A short piece of writing that gives information or the author's opinion on a subject. Can be focused around fiction or non-fiction.
Fantasy	A story with impossible events taking place, such as talking animals or magical powers.
Mystery	A story about a puzzling event that isn't solved until the end of the story.
Realistic fiction	A story with made-up characters and events that could really happen now.
Biography	A story of a real person's life written by another person.
Autobiography	The story of a real person's life that is written by that same person.
Historical fiction	A fictional story with real and made-up characters that takes place during a historical time.
Science fiction	A story that blends technology from the future with scientific fact or fiction.

Let me stress that if I am working on a poetry unit of study, all students are reading poetry during the independent reading time. I also will use poetry for my mini-lesson and the read-aloud. The chart below is kept inside the students' reading folders. The genre charts (above) that are posted around the room, as well as the ongoing chart from Chapter 3 (see Table 3.1) helps this record-keeping of genres to remain independent.

As a side note, my class does take the time to look at the book ratings on *Amazon.com*. I explain how I am a "one click" connoisseur and that the star ratings do drive my purchasing choices. Also, I have cut this chart into strips so that students can pull a strip, record the information, and place it under the correct heading on a bulletin board. That gives the class a quick look at what genre is the most widely read in our room. Because I am a little OCD, I have each strip on different colored copy paper based on the genre. It adds to the visual and makes the bulletin board colorful and inviting. Here is a sample of my color choices for the genres:

Mystery: dark yellow

Myth: light purple

Folk tales: light green

Fantasy: red

Poetry: dark green

Taking a Genre Walk

Students love exploring different genres, and the texts teachers choose to let them explore in the genre walk do not need to be books. I scout through *Storyworks*, *Highlights*, and some of my older editions of *Cricket* magazine, and copy text samples of each genre in the chart above. I am always on the look-out for examples, and place them in labeled baskets when I find them. If teachers work together, it is easier to create a collection. This "walk" can be used to introduce the different genres, help students decide what type to check out at the library, or just refresh their minds on the different characteristics of each genre. Because I have about twenty short samples from magazines in each basket, this activity can be used all year. Don't forget about well-written student samples, those are perfect in each genre basket.

Here is how the genre basket works: Students pair up and draw a genre type from a basket where I have written each type on different strips of paper. There may be more than one pair of students at a genre basket, and that is fine. Each pair of students selects a sample and then moves away from the

Figure 6.2 Chart in students' notebooks

Name_____

Ranking * Okay ** Really Good *** You Have to Read This!!

Title_____

Author_____

Date_____ Genre_____

Ranking:_____

Title_____

Author_____

Date_____ Genre_____

Ranking:_____

Title_____

Author_____

Date_____ Genre_____

Ranking:_____

Title_____

Author_____

Date_____ Genre_____

Ranking:_____

Title_____

Author_____

Date_____ Genre_____

Ranking:_____

Title_____

Author_____

Date_____ Genre_____

Ranking:_____

basket to a working area. On task cards, I have questions written, and the goal is for the students to read, record answers based on what they read, and then return the genre strip to the basket and grab another one. After several rotations, we put everything up, reflect on our findings, and move into my mini-lesson for the day. This activity could also serve as my mini-lesson for the day.

Figure 6.3 Genre task cards

Card #1

What genre is the selection?

Card #2

What kinds of characters are in the selection?

Card #3

Describe the setting...

Card #4

What other clues (besides character and setting) did the text provide you about the type of genre you selected?

Card #5

Write a one minute summary/review of the text you (and your partner) just read.

Teaching Students to be Pros at Prose

Let's take a moment to look a little closer at the prose, poetry, and drama. Prose is a form of language that has a grammatical and natural flow of speech rather than a rhythmic one. Normal everyday speech is spoken in prose and most people think in prose. It is basically the standard style of writing that students come into contact with each day (literature, speeches, broadcasts, etc.) One of my favorite quotes by Mother Teresa is an example of prose: "The poor are very great people. They can teach us so many things." The language is simple, direct, and leaves the reader with a message. That is not to say that prose writing does not have the elements of craft language that were covered in Chapter 5. On the contrary, it does; the rhyming and rhythmic nature may not be found but creativity certainly is.

Effective Teaching Strategies for Prose

1. Read
2. Write
3. Discuss
4. Integrate technology

There are several types of prose:

1. *Nonfiction prose*—biographies and essays
2. *Fictional prose*—chapter books, novels, stories
3. *Heroic prose*—legends and tall tales
4. *Prose poetry*—poetry, usually written in the narrative, but not written in verse, unlike much of the poetry students read.

Teaching prose means teaching reading with comprehension. Teachers often ask students to name the basic story elements of what they have read: setting, character, problem, and solution. As readers mature in their understanding of these basic elements, teachers want students to read with more depth of meaning and understanding. Students gain this deeper understanding by interpreting the author's purpose, inferring themes and internal messages and making personal connections. The key is to use a variety of strategies to keep students motivated and interested. The simplest way for me to do that is to make sure I select mentor texts that appeal to my students and that I have studied.

Teaching Students to Interpret Prose Orally

According to Jim Trelese, "The most common mistake in reading aloud is reading too fast." Encourage students to read slowly enough for the reader to build mental pictures, also making sure that the text level is appropriate for the reader. The level should be independent or upper instructional level.

Recommended Mentor Texts for Elements of Prose

We Planted a Tree by Diane Muldrow

The Longest Night by Marion Diane Bauer

Owl Moon by Jane Yolen

The Ghost-Eye Tree by Bill Martin Jr.

Poetry

Poetry is one of my favorite genres to teach, and the students love it. I begin the year with a poem a week and let the students practice coding the text in a close read. I like to keep these weekly poems thematic or seasonally based to build the background knowledge and connections of students. This weekly invitation is an excellent way to spark interest in the genre as well as introduce vocabulary, word choice, and visualization found in poetry. Then when we begin a longer unit of study, the students are aware of the basics, and ready for a deeper study. One area I like to focus on in my study is the rhythm and the rhyme.

Table 6.3 Vocabulary for Poetry

VOCABULARY	MEANING	EXAMPLE
verse		
repetition		
imagery		
rhyme		
foot		
rhythm		
meter		

The Rhythm of Poetry

The first time I set up a poetry unit, I looked more at the "outside" perspective of the reader. In other words, I focused more on the poetic devices. The conversations were pretty good, but the poetry the students wrote was lacking. Then I realized that students would connect to the fact that poetry is basically a song. All of my students love music, and when I asked them what made them like a particular song, they said "the beat." My brain stopped for a moment and took this in . . . so if I start my poetry unit on the beat or the rhythm and not so much the content (remember in Chapter 5 when I explained how my teacher killed the Emily Dickinson poem for me? I may have been a little guilty of that myself when starting out), then I will see more creativity in the poems the students write. Teachers know the importance of students writing about what they have read, or similar. So my goal was to get "to the beat!"

So my second attempt at the unit began from the "inside" view, with the making of the poem, not the finished piece. That is not to say that the students did not read poems in their entirety, but it was the rhythm and beat we looked at first, attempting to understand and then recreate it. I would plan a second or third read of the poems and, at that point, get to the content, the word choice, message, visualizing moments, etc. Reading aloud is one of the best ways to get "inside" a poem, because the stress and tone of voice are really dependent on meaning, and the reader must understand the poem on a personal level to read it well.

Since students like to move around, we do, and the students love it. I ask for them to each bring in the lyrics of a song that is popular on the radio. It has to be appropriate of course and all teachers know that a conversation and quick note home explaining the assignment to parents will alleviate most issues. One song that some students brought in was *Fireworks* by Katy Perry. I distributed copies of the song, we sang it, and then we looked at the beat. Having students clap out the syllables in the words, count the words in each line, and look at the repeating central lyric was an excellent way to start the unit of study. The song lyrics the students brought in became my read-alouds and the focus of my mini-lessons. The lyrics were also posted on a "We've Got the Beat" bulletin board (and yes, I did have to introduce the oldie but goody "We've Got the Beat" by the Go-Gos—the students loved it!), and the students wrote their own poetic lyrics using the same or some of the syllabic patterns (beat) from the song choices. I even went back to the "old school" method of counting syllables in words, to clap it out, or touch your chin, when a separation of a word is noted. This practice was also incorporated into our weekly spelling words, ("How many syllables does each word have?") so that students were immersed in the awareness of the words and rhythms and syllabic patterns used in song lyrics. Then it was time to start looking at written poems by the greats: Jack Prelutsky and Shel Silverstein. I am not suggesting that we did not also look closely at Robert Frost or Walt Whitman; I just wanted to let the students see that poetry can be silly with a purpose, and then look at how poems were also serious and emotional. Below are eight activities students enjoy but that also review or introduce the elements of rhythm and rhyme. Because students in grades 2–5 have a grasp on rhyming words, I looked closer at rhythm in poetry.

Rhythm

1. Teach rhythm first. I also ask my music teacher to work with my students and tie in how syllables, and accenting of syllables, play a part in music as well. Start with your students' names. Put several 2-syllable and 3-syllable names on the board, and scan them to show where the accent falls in each, using/for an accented syllable and – for an unaccented syllable. Then have students count the number of syllables in each name. They love looking at their own name and will often beg to tear apart their middle name, their last name, the names of their pets, etc.

Annette	–/	(2)
Andy	/–	(2)
Mary Lou	– –/	(3)
Dominick	/– –	(3)
Belinda	–/–	(3)

The advantage of starting with students' names is that it makes them feel personally involved in a kind of word-play at the handclapping, foot-tapping level that still doesn't demand much from them emotionally or intellectually. Let those demands come later.

2. Break up the class into groups of students whose names scan the same way, and ask them to list words and phrases they can think of that scan like their names. Have each group put up on the board, and tap out, several items from their list, and have the rest of the class make corrections, if necessary. This is a good introduction to *accentual-syllabic* meter: meter that takes into consideration both the number of syllables per line and whether certain

syllables are accented or not. Another variation is for the teacher to display one word at a time on their own list, and if the syllable is accented, the students stand up, if it is not, they sit down. I still use the tried and true dictionary set in my classroom. Giving students the chance to look through the dictionary to self-check their determination of the number of syllables as well as the accented/not accented parts of words is an excellent reinforcement.

3. Give your students opening lines to poems and let them add three or four more in exactly the same meter. Don't bother with rhyming, or with serious meaning; nonsense verse is fine, so long as they enjoy it and practice shifting syllables around to achieve different sound patterns. To add a little variety, offer each row a different opening line, or offer the whole class several and let each student decide for themselves which one to try. Vary your openings, so they'll get to practice as many different metrical patterns as possible.

4. Read aloud some strongly rhythmical nursery rhymes—"Pease Porridge Hot" is a good choice—and clap your hands at the accented syllables to show that their number is constant, but the number of unaccented syllables varies from line to line. This is a good way to introduce *accentual verse*, which is fun to try, and easy, because students are concerned only with the accents per line.

5. Distribute examples of cinquains, haiku, senryu or tanka poems, to help introduce *syllabic verse*. This is an easy meter, because the students only have to count so many syllables per line, whether they are accented or not. Here is a review of the syllable requirements for each type of poem:

- The *cinquain* has five lines: two syllables in the first, four in the second, six in the third, eight in the fourth, and two in the last.
- The *tanka* has five lines: it is like a haiku with two 7-syllable lines added to it. The *tanka* may deal with a broader range of themes, including events in human life.
- The *haiku* usually deals with some aspect of nature, and works by suggesting more than it says. The language is simple, with few, if any, figures of speech. Typically the reader is asked to observe something and arrive at some unspoken insight of their own.
- The *senryu,* which is metrically just like the haiku, generally deals with human phenomena rather than strictly natural ones.

6. After your students have tried writing cinquains, haiku, senryu and tanka poems, ask them to invent a syllabic pattern of their own. Put up as many samples as possible, and read them aloud. Invite students to name their invented forms. Encourage them to experiment with each other's new forms. Tell them that the famous poetic forms we have today, such as the sonnet and the limerick, were also invented by individuals—just like them.

7. Add rhyme to the mix. Put up several of your students' names on the board, being sure to include some 1-syllable, 2-syllable and 3-syllable names. Invite the class to think of rhymes for each, for example:

Billy/silly

Bella/fella

Kim/gem

8. Explain the use of letters to designate rhymes, and show them how the *rhyme scheme* works in specific poems. Introduce the limerick as an example of a short rhymed form, and assign them the writing of a limerick. They will probably attempt more than one: the limerick is habit-forming. The wonderful thing about using limericks is that both the rhythm and rhyme can be looked at closely. Many limericks follow an 8, 8, 5, 5, 8 syllable rhythm and an AABBA rhyming pattern. But let me caution that as long as the students are close to the syllable rhythm, that is fine. Writing poetry, like anything else, is a process. Here is an example that my class helped compose. We included the syllables and the designated letters to show the rhyme scheme.

There once was a gentle fellow (A) (8)

Who liked to be calm and mellow (A) (8)

So one day he went (B) (5)

Inside of a tent (B) (5)

And started to play the cello! (A) (8)

Digging Drama

Drama is meant to be performed rather than read. Typically we call the texts plays or reader's theaters. Unfortunately this is one genre that is usually given the least amount of time in class. Why? Time. Since dramas are meant to be acted out in front of an audience, extra preparation will have to be done. But to me, it is well worth it. One area that my fourth graders come to me struggling with is fluency. When they read, the words are often unemotional and lacking the voice and flow that makes listening a pleasure. With the onset of drama in the CCSS, teachers are giving this type of reading a new chance.

Vocabulary for Drama

Students need to be familiar with the academic vocabulary that will help them determine the differences between the genres of prose, poetry, and drama. The convenient thing about using actual movie scripts (more information below) is that examples of these terms are right within the scripts so that students can "see them in action!"

- stage directions
- act
- scene
- subplot
- narrator (ties in with point of view)

Looking Closer at Movie Scripts

One "newbie" I have added to my collection of genres is movie scripts. If you search for kid-friendly movie scripts on the Internet, be prepared to see Frozen and Aladdin, and many many more. I print these scripts off and the class uses them for (1) a reader's theater, (2) to discuss point of view, (3) character perspective, and of course, we watch parts of the actual movies and the students can use their scripts to follow along. If I have a picture book of the same title, we compare how the movie and the book are similar or different. Then a quick vote of which was best is always in order. Movie scripts are one of the neatest additions to my curriculum. After a workshop this summer, when I introduced the use of movie scripts to a group of teachers, the second and third grade teachers let me know that basic story elements would also be taught using them. Here is a tidbit of a script I found on www.imsbd.com/scripts/. I could go on and on about how to use movie scripts in the classroom.

An Excerpt from *Aladdin*

(GAZEEM starts to approach the lion's mouth, which forms the entrance to the cave. He chuckles as he goes.)

IAGO: Awk, the lamp! Awk, the lamp!

(Now that IAGO and JAFAR are alone, IAGO opens up in normal English.)

Jeez, where'd ya dig this bozo up?

(JAFAR puts his finger to his lips and shushes him. GAZEEM reaches the cave, but is blown away by the roar of the cave's speaking.)

CAVE: Who disturbs my slumber?
GAZEEM: It is I, Gazeem, a humble thief.
CAVE: Know this. Only one may enter here. One whose worth lies far within. A diamond in the rough.

(GAZEEM turns to JAFAR with a questioning look.)

JAFAR: What are you waiting for? Go on!

(GAZEEM hesitates, then moves one foot inside the cave. With great apprehension, he plants his foot down. Nothing happens. Relieved, he begins his trek again. Then another roar comes. He turns back, but the lion's mouth slams shut and the dune collapses back to normal. All that are left are JAFAR, IAGO, and the two separated halves of the medallion.)

CAVE: Seek thee out, the diamond in the rough.

Point of View

Who is speaking in the stories that we read to our students and in the stories they read? The "voice" readers hear is the point of view. If you teach with the 6 Traits (a nationally recognized model for writing instruction) in the writer's workshop, the trait of voice ties in nicely with point of view. Voice is considered the "personality" of the writer and in reading; this voice is the lens that readers use to discover who is telling the story. My students helped me create an anchor chart to get the unit of study rolling.

Also, a hand-out for the reader's notebook is useful for students.

Table 6.4 Point of View Definition Target Words

POINT OF VIEW	DEFINITION	TARGET WORDS
First person	This is told from the point of view of one of the characters.	I, we, me, my
Second person (rarely used other than in "how-to" or technical writing)	The narrator addresses YOU, the reader.	you, yours
Third person	The narrator is NOT part of the story.	he, she, they, a character's name

First Person

When the author writes in first person, they use words such as *I, we, me, and my*. This is called first-person narration. When my students write personal narratives or memoirs, they are writing from this point of view. When I am reading aloud a story in first person, any time the students hear and see (I read all stories and texts using the document camera) the pronoun "I" they hold up their pointing finger. We lovingly say "because 'I' is always number 1." When the pronouns "me" or "my" are in the text, they point and touch their chests with the pointing finger, "because it's all 'mine'." Sometimes the silliest off-the-top-of-our-head strategies stick with the students more than anything else.

Mentor Texts for First Person

Once Upon a Cool Motorcycle Dude by Kevin O'Malley
Help Me Mr. Mutt: Expert Answers for Dogs with People Problems by Janet Stevens and Susan Stevens Crummel
Diary of a Worm by Doreen Cronin
With Love, Little Red Hen by Alma Flor Ada
Birdhouse for Rent by Harriet Ziefert
My Big Dog by Janet Stevens and Susan Stevens Crummel
Crocodile by Fred Marcellino
A Hey, Little Ant by Phillip and Hannah Hoose
Somebody and the Three Blairs by Marilyn Tolhurst
The True Story of the Three Little Pigs by Jon Scieszka

Figure 6.4 Narrative viewpoints

First-person point of view

- The narrator is one of the characters in the story.
- First-person pronouns, such as I, me, my, and mine are used in telling the story.
- Since the narrator is a character in the story, he/she may not be completely reliable.
- We find out only what this character knows, thinks, and witnesses.

Third-person objective

- The narrator is not a character in the story.
- Third-person pronouns such as he, his, she, hers, it, its, they, and them are used in telling the story.
- The narrator is an observer who can only tell what is said and done.
- The narrator cannot see into the minds of any of the characters.
- We find out only what the characters say and do.

Third-person limited

- The narrator is not a character in the story.
- Third-person pronouns such as he, his, she, hers, it, its, they, and them are used in telling the story.
- The narrator tells the story from the vantage point of one character.
- The narrator can see into this character's mind, but not any of the other characters.
- We find out only what this character does, knows, thinks, and witnesses.

Third-person omniscient

- The narrator is not a character in the story.
- Third-person pronouns such as he, his, she, hers, it, its, they, and them are used in telling the story.
- The narrator is all-knowing, and can see into the minds of all of the characters. The narrator can also report what is said and done.
- We find out what all of the characters do, feel, think, and witness.

Second-person point of view

- Second-person pronouns such as you, your, and yours are used.
- Most stories are not told in second person. It is reserved for items of personal address, such as a letter or a how-to type text.

Third Person

When the author writes in third person, a character in the story is the narrator. There are three types of third-person point of view. My students understand the following L-O-O-k acronym: It reminds them to "look" for evidence to help determine which type of third-person point of view they are reading.

1. **Limited**—The narrator focuses on the thoughts and feelings of only one character.
2. **Omniscient**—The narrator is ALL-knowing and can tell the thoughts and feelings of all of the characters.
3. **Objective**—The narrator reports only facts and events as a neutral observer.

Thought-provoking Activities for Point of View

1. Identifying Multiple Views

For this activity, each student cuts out a picture from a magazine or catalogue. This picture is glued to the left side of their organizer then, independently or in pairs, the students creat a text about the picture in the first- or third-person (all three types) point of view. I want to stress that we do not ignore the second-person point of view. When the students write "how to" papers or persuasive pieces, the use of second person to address the reader is stressed. Table 6.5 is a graphic organizer students use.

2. The Torn Pants

This is not a new activity. It has been around for some time, but the students enjoy it. I recently ran across it again in Ruth Culham's book, *Using Picture Books to Teach Writing with the Traits* (Scholastic, 2014). The idea is to give the students an incident regarding a rip in a pair of pants, and then they write from the point of view or perspective of several "witnesses" to the incident, including the pants. I have students get into groups and write from the point of view of one of the following:

- the pants
- the student (wearing the pants)
- the principal
- the teacher
- another student who witnessed the rip

Table 6.5 Identifying Multiple Views

PICTURE	Perspective
	First-person point of view
	Third-person limited
	Third-person omniscient
	Third-person objective

* I do review how perspective and point of view are similar yet also different. A perspective is a particular attitude towards something.

3. Analyzing Point of View

I am a fan of ways to organize students' thinking. This organizer (Table 6.6) does the trick for point of view. The objective is for students to concentrate on the view of one of the main characters and then infer what the author's point of view of the story was while the story was being written; in other words, the students are thinking backwards.

Table 6.6 Analyzing Point of View

Character's worldview:	Writer's worldview:
Details:	Details:
Conclusions:	Conclusions:

4. Point of View Review

Letting students create task cards for reviewing point of view serves two purposes: it creates a higher level thinking activity for the student writing the cards and an excellent review for the student practicing with the cards. To begin, I ask for each student to write one type of point of view on the front of an index card and then an example on the back. I make sure that all types of "views" are represented. Typically I have time for each student to create two review cards. These cards are used in a station, as a quick whole class review, or even as a game with teams. As the answer is on one side and the text on the other, self-checking is simple. Here is an example of what might be written on a card.

Figure 6.5 Sample card

Front of Card

Third Person Limited

Back of Card *(If time permits, students can illustrate the text they created.)*

Joanne was so excited to take a trip! She packed her things and began her adventure!

5. The Delapidated House

This activity is also excellent for teaching empathy as well as perspective. I find several old "run-down" houses from the Internet. I print them off either to use in groups, or display one on the document camera for all of the students to use. Then I ask for students to fold a piece of notebook paper like a hotdog bun (vertical) and write POV #1 (neighbor) on the left side. I do not reveal what will be on the right side yet. I do not want to affect the "voice". Students then write from the point of view of the neighbor. I will be honest, sometimes the students are pretty "vocal" in their disapproval of the conditions they must live beside. Their voices are often a touch accusing and I allow this, as long as it does not cross the line of disrespectful. The class share what they have written. Then I ask for the students to write POV#2 (resident) on the right side of the T-chart. Now they must write from the point of view of the person who lives in the run-down house. It is amazing to hear the voice change, and to watch the students become empathetic to reasons why this house has become run-down. Often reasons such as cancer or death of a spouse are used to serve as the rationale for why the conditions have become what they have. This point of view is also shared among students and the activity usually sparks a deep discussion.

Choice Board

R	E	A	D
Describe the genre of poetry. What structures make up poems? How do poems differ from prose?	Read a play. How do you know it is a play? In your answer include the structural elements that let you know this is a play.	Explain the difference between prose (story), drama, and a poem.	Read a poem. Write a similar version of the poem using your own words.
Define the following terminology: stage directions, scene, act, and cast.	What do the terms have in common? After reading a chapter book, choose a chapter and turn it into a scene of a play.	Define the following terminology: verse, meter, rhythm, line, and stanza.	What do these terms have in common? After reading a play, summarize it. Include these terms in your summary: cast, description, setting, dialogue, stage directions.

Closing Thoughts

Teaching reading is a passion that most teachers have. We embrace the multitude of skills and standards that are aligned with the curriculum. If teachers work together, across all grade levels and share information as well as advice, our job gets a little easier. It is my goal, with this book, to help teachers feel a little more connected to the Common Core Literature Standards and claim ownership over the curriculum in their classrooms. Teachers hold the key. I have never been so proud of our profession, not the state requirements or the abundance of testing, rather the way teachers hold on tight and don't give up when the pendulum swings one way or the other. We understand it will swing again and again, and as we hold true to why we entered the profession—to touch the minds of students—then that pendulum can twirl a complete 360 and we will still walk into our classrooms, close the doors, and teach our hearts out. After all, that is why we became teachers in the first place.

For Product Safety Concerns and Information please contact our EU representative GPSR@taylorandfrancis.com
Taylor & Francis Verlag GmbH, Kaufingerstraße 24, 80331 München, Germany

www.ingramcontent.com/pod-product-compliance
Lightning Source LLC
Chambersburg PA
CBHW080937300426
44115CB00017B/2848